**Second Ed**

MW00561218

# Coaching
# the Veer Offense

**George Thole and Jerry Foley**

COACHES
CHOICE™

ISBN: 978-1-60679-013-7
Library of Congress Control Number: 2008936004
Book layout: Studio J Art & Design
Cover design: Studio J Art & Design
Front cover photo: Scott Ertle, Stillwater Gazette

Coaches Choice
P.O. Box 1828
Monterey, CA 93942
www.coacheschoice.com

# Dedication

This book is dedicated to the Stillwater Area High School Football Staff, 1971–1999.
Sherm Danielson
Donn Drommerhausen
Mark Elmer
Steve Forseth
Gary Gustafson
Scott Hoffman
Dick Klein
Dennis Meyer
Larry Miller
Mike Pavlovich
Tom Rasmussen
Darrell Salmi
Eric Thole
Dick Weinberger


Gene "Taco" Bealka, trainer
Dick Schmidt, equipment manager
C. J. Knoche, athletic director


## In Memory
Ken Anderson
Bob Choinere
Tom Foley
Tom Juhl
Dana Miller
Peter Miller Jr.
Dave Pedersen
Buddy Richert
Rob Ries
Joe "Sam" Samuelson
Rob Uppgren

# Acknowledgments

We wish to thank the following individuals for their contributions of time and talent to help make this book project become a reality.

Darlene Foley and Karen Thole, our dedicated wives

Mike Foley, advisor

Todd Fultz, National Sports Gallery
   Cover painting and marketing

Rosemary Jensen, proofreader

Doug Meythaler, artist, "Pony Pride"

Joe Samuelson, instructional photos

Pat St. Claire, graphic design and project coordinator

Amy Thole and Rose Ramirez, typists

Stillwater Area High School, Minnesota Class 5A
   Enrollment Grades 10–12: 2100 Students

We also want to express our gratitude to the local media, photographers, and individuals who have contributed photos of the Ponies in action and in victory over the years.

# Foreword

Playing varsity football for the Stillwater Ponies during the '89 and '90 seasons were lessons I could apply to life. As I often look back and analyze Coach Thole and Foley's instructional techniques and motivation, I have reached several conclusions. In that regard, Maslow's hierarchy of needs provides a format for my thinking. The only significant difference between my perception and Maslow's actual hierarchy is that winning in football is substituted for self-actualization.

Winning was paramount in Stillwater football. In order to achieve this objective, however, a multitude of things needed to fall into place. Players needed to understand first and foremost why it was important to win. This concept may seem basic, but Stillwater had a history of winning in football, and had a town supporting the team's performance on the field every Friday night. This theme of winning was constantly reinforced in every practice. Practice served as an avenue for the coaches to harness the players' desires to win.

The coaches also had a need to bring all members of the team together to form a bond with each other. This step was done by confronting the players with intense physical and mental challenges at practice every day. The start of season brought exhausting practices in the morning and afternoon, with an occasional shorter practice in between the two. Amidst the sweating of players came the numbing voice of Coach Thole, demanding the need for proper execution. The need for players to execute their responsibilities properly was never overlooked. For example, if one player failed in the execution of an option to the right side, all 11 members of that unit would run the play again until it was executed properly. I remember seeing players break down into tears in the midst of Coach Thole's words of "encouragement."

When you rely on others to get your job done, a certain bond is formed between players. That bond served as the basis for achieving the common goal of winning. Complacency was not an option. Improvement was a daily activity. As such, all came down to making players responsible for their individual actions. If a player was not on board with the goals of the team, that individual was removed from the unit.

The aforementioned approach can also be applied in my life as an officer in the United States Air Force. For example, it is a challenge to supervise a group of co-workers. As such, it is imperative when asking someone to accomplish a task that the person being addressed understands why his job is important to the organization. Much like the aforementioned diagram, individuals who are associated with a company or team need a clear picture of the direction their organization is going. It is also necessary for the leader of an organization to develop a bond with the individuals for whom he is responsible. Whether this situation involves work or play, the need to develop a bond of trust is crucial. Accomplishing these actions empowers people to do their job in alignment with the organization.

Getting people aligned with the organization's purpose for existence is no different than it was for Stillwater football. Pony football made me realize that once a team is in alignment with a common goal, that team is like a freight train. A powerful and aligned train cannot be derailed. The success that coaches Thole and Foley had with Pony football started with molding individuals into a team. Once the team was formed, it was difficult to knock the Ponies from the top of their gridiron perch.

Glenn Harris
'91 Ponies Co-Captain, All-Conference, 1990
Four Year Letterman—Baseball at U.S.A.F. Academy
Major, United States Air Force, Pentagon, Washington, D.C.

# **Contents**

# Preface

I first met George Thole in the spring of 1971 when he was hired as the head football coach at Stillwater High School. I had come to Stillwater at the beginning of the 1963–64 school year after spending my initial two-year teaching/coaching experience at Lincoln High School in Thief River Falls, Minnesota. I paid my dues as a rookie coach under the guidance of such stalwarts as Joe Mrkonich in Thief River Falls along with the late Joe Samuelson and Carver Fouks in Stillwater. Carver gave me my first opportunity to coach at the varsity level and to assist in formulating the offensive game plan. For the lessons and insights gained under the direction of these dedicated men, I am forever grateful. By the time George arrived on our campus, I was a varsity assistant in the football program and the head hockey coach for the Pony icemen.

## Foley About Thole: Early Beginnings

George came to Stillwater from a very successful football program at Richfield High where he was the Spartans' defensive coordinator. Previously, while working on a master's degree, he served as a graduate assistant coach at the University of Minnesota under then head coach, Murray Warmath.

Thole began his football coaching career with unheard-of success as the rookie head coach at Central High School in Casselton, North Dakota. In his first season, he led a team tabbed to finish at the bottom of the conference to a perfect 9-0 record and a conference championship. Although a tough act to follow, his next two teams finished their respective seasons undefeated, giving him a phenomenal record of 27-0 and three consecutive conference championships in his first three years as a head coach.

In the first year at Stillwater High School, George installed what could be called a multiple type offense. It featured a mix of power and finesse football mingled with the option game. Formations included I-back sets, power I, and split-back sets, run from pro, two tight ends, flex, and twin set formations. Due to limited talent and lack of numbers, our goal was to control the football as long as possible by utilizing the play clock, snapping the ball at the last possible second. We believed as long as we had the football, it would be difficult for our opponents to score. It played out well, and the players were able to adjust to a new system. We were competitive that first year and were never blown out of the water, but due to our limitations on both sides of the ball, we finished the 1971 season with a 3-6 record, and in coach-speak, we did manage to be "in" every game.

The 1972 season saw our football program improve in every facet of the game offensively and defensively along with special-teams play. However, we were still chasing the "big dogs" in the conference. We played solid defense and controlled the football satisfactorily, but were inconsistent in putting points on the scoreboard. Although the season ended with a disappointing 3-4-2 win-loss record, it was evident that the players were getting stronger both physically and mentally and were beginning to come together as a team. We began to experiment, on a very limited scale, with the split-back veer.

Under the leadership and direction of the head coach, cohesiveness developed within our staff, and the 1973 season was a turnaround year for the Stillwater High School football program. Following a somewhat inauspicious start, having dropped the first two games by narrow margins, we regrouped and reeled off seven straight victories in the strong St. Paul Suburban Football Conference. Arguably, at the end of the season, the Ponies were one of the top prep football teams in the metro area, probably in the state. Again, the defense was rock-solid, and the offense was effective enough to control the football while playing a significant role in a successful campaign. Our attack was more power-oriented football than option-oriented, but we continued experimenting with the concept of the veer offense, employing split backs and twin receivers. The 7-2 season record was the highest finish and the most victories enjoyed by a Pony football team dating back to the 1953 season.

The 6-3 record during the 1974 season, although a winning record, was disappointing because our expectations and our goals were much higher. By that point, we were using the split-back veer as a part of our multiple, mixed attack. Statistics showed that over the past two seasons we were winning the majority of our games and were controlling our opponents. Our victories were by scores of 21-7, 14-0, 28-14, 7-0, and the like. We were winning football games, but were not blowing anyone out of the tank. Game analysis and films indicated that although the veer was part of our total offensive package, in tight situations we often tended to play it safe and stay with our power I and related formations with which we were comfortable.

## Bayport Right

In the spring of 1975, George informed the staff that he was burning the offensive playbooks and throwing everything out except the twin-veer attack. To say that this was shocking news is an understatement. We had been running the veer in games, but only when convenient and within our comfort zone when everything was clicking. With the game on the line, it was easy to revert to the steady old reliable, 03 power, 04 power, iso left or right, power sweep," and such.

His message to me was that we would be exclusively a veer-option football team. I was further informed that we would have exactly three inside running plays, two triple options, along with three additional options to get the ball on the perimeter. Our attack would be a run-oriented offense, combined with play-action and sprint-out passes to keep the defenses from loading up on the running game.

In the previous seasons while experimenting with the veer attack, I was elated when our quarterback and dive back managed to arrive at the mesh point simultaneously. Making a clean handoff without leaving the ball on the ground only added to my pleasure. It was sobering news for me to learn that this approach, indeed, was to be our sole offensive scheme. It did make for a very interesting and busy summer for George and me as we prepared to install the split-back veer as our basic offense in the coming fall of 1975.

Thole's rationale in installing the veer attack proved prophetic when he said, "As long as we have multiple sets and formations and rely on power football, we will never be a true option team." We would continue to win our share of games, but because of inconsistencies in scoring points, we could lose the close game here and there, thus depriving us of the ultimate goal, that of being champions.

## Afton/Withrow

In order to involve the entire community while enjoining all facets of the St. Croix Valley into the Stillwater football program, names of local areas were used to designate our offensive and defensive sets. Familiar terms like Bayport, Afton, and Withrow became commonplace in our vocabulary as we introduced the newly christened offense, the "Bayport veer." The goal was to create excitement and pride in the program, thus encouraging and expanding community involvement.

In the interim, Thole and I developed eyestrain from reading everything we could lay our hands on having anything to do with split-back veer football. We attended clinics and picked the brains of anyone and everyone who had any connection with the offense. College coaches like Lou Holtz, Don Morton, and Jim Wacker, who had great success running the veer offense, became excellent sources of information for us as we adapted our attack to fit the needs and skill levels of the high school athletes available to us. Many of their thoughts, ideas, terminologies, and methods were of great value to us as we worked to perfect our system. As a coach, I have borrowed, begged, and pilfered anything and everything I could use to enable me to be as effective as possible in teaching young football players how to play the game. As the date signifying the beginning of the 1975 football drew nigh, we were eager and well prepared to install the "new look" offense at Stillwater High School.

## Run It Again

By design, we are an execution-oriented offense, and as such, put tremendous emphasis on the player's ability to carry out individual assignments to the letter. With the veer offense, footwork, mesh points, and landmarks are precise and unchanging. Each of the movements of the quarterback, dive back, and running back are carefully choreographed and measured. In turn, the blocking rules of the linemen are exact, constant, and involve zoning the playside and scooping the backside. Precision and timing are the benchmarks used to measure the success or failure of the system. It is not necessarily the system that equates to success, but rather the execution of said system.

Repetition and strict attention to detail are absolutely necessary in perfecting the read offense. The outside veer and the split veer are the only true triple options incorporated in the Bayport veer attack. Part of our success in running the triple is attributed to the fact that we have simplified the rules for the quarterback in making the reads. By limiting the number of decisions to be made, we increase the percentages leading to successful completion of the play. During practice, the majority of our individual period for quarterbacks and running backs is spent running option drills under game conditions and against a variety of defensive looks. If you are an option football team, then you had better run option football every day at practice.

As a coach, it is vital not only to believe thoroughly in what you are teaching, but also to instill these beliefs in your players. Coach the hell out of the minute details and attack your subject matter "hammer and tongs." Believe in yourself, enjoy the moment, then "run it again!"

## To Veer or Not to Veer

A brief look at the results of our program after having run the twin veer over a period of 25 seasons (1975-1999) is revealing and convincing (Figure 1). Having never been a great proponent of the statistical aspects of the game and all that they entail, these numbers are difficult to ignore and are quite meaningful. Statistics do not always tell the complete story and may even be misleading to the interpreter. The intention here is to pass on to the reader the results of a well-designed, thoroughly coached system, which just happened to be the twin-veer offense.

In the fall of 1975, the first full season of running the veer as our exclusive offense, the team finished the year undefeated with a perfect 12-0 record, capturing its first football conference championship since 1953 and its first ever state high school football championship. To say that our success was based solely on the veer attack is simplistic, but gives credibility to the system and to what we were all about. It did prove

| Stillwater Veer Offense Per-Game Averages 1973–1999 | | | | |
|---|---|---|---|---|
| Year | Win-Loss | Points Scored | Yards Gained | Average Per Play |
| 1973 | 7-2 | 22.0 | 273.4 | 5.2 |
| 1974 | 6-3 | 19.1 | 305.1 | 6.0 |
| 1975 | 12-0 | 25.3 | 277.2 | 6.4 |
| 1976 | 8-1 | 29.7 | 319.9 | 6.6 |
| 1977 | 11-1 | 27.3 | 322.5 | 6.0 |
| 1978 | 10-1 | 31.6 | 366.1 | 6.6 |
| 1979 | 9-1 | 39.5 | 366.4 | 7.3 |
| 1980 | 7-2 | 18.0 | 277.7 | 6.6 |
| 1981 | 7-2 | 12.5 | 226.0 | 4.4 |
| 1982 | 11-1 | 24.1 | 281.6 | 6.1 |
| 1983 | 8-2 | 25.6 | 265.8 | 5.7 |
| 1984 | 11-3 | 23.5 | 281.1 | 5.4 |
| 1985 | 11-1 | 34.6 | 332.5 | 6.2 |
| 1986 | 11-2 | 28.4 | 305.5 | 6.0 |
| 1987 | 10-3 | 24.6 | 321.8 | 6.2 |
| 1988 | 11-2 | 39.0 | 351.2 | 6.6 |
| 1989 | 10-4 | 27.2 | 316.1 | 5.9 |
| 1990 | 10-3 | 21.0 | 256.9 | 5.3 |
| 1991 | 7-5 | 21.5 | 292.9 | 5.8 |
| 1992 | 11-2 | 32.2 | 355.5 | 6.3 |
| 1993 | 10-2 | 36.8 | 407.5 | 7.5 |
| 1994 | 8-3 | 32.5 | 323.6 | 6.6 |
| 1995 | 14-0 | 34.1 | 300.7 | 5.6 |
| 1996 | 12-1 | 28.8 | 292.9 | 5.8 |
| 1997 | 7-4 | 16.6 | 234.6 | 4.2 |
| 1998 | 7-3 | 24.7 | 272.5 | 4.9 |
| 1999 | 5-5 | 23.3 | 300.0 | 5.0 |

Figure 1. Stillwater veer offense per-game averages

to be a successful testing ground for the embryonic beginnings of the Bayport veer offense and a harbinger of what was to become a devastating scoring machine that dominated its opponents over the next 25 seasons.

Offensively, we did not blow our opponents away in 1975, but were able to become established as a viable option football team. It gave us a foundation to build upon as we developed the nuances and intricate aspects of the option game. By trial and error, we were able to "tweak" the offense and adapt it to the personnel available at our level of competition.

Without expounding in a litany, or a year-by-year account of the happenings between the 1975 and 1999 seasons, suffice it to say that this offense averaged 32 points and 332 yards per game, while attaining an amazing 9.23 victories per season over a 25-year span. It also was a major factor in producing 19 championship years, including four state championships, 13 conference championships, 12 sectional championships, two state runners up finishes, and a record 18 appearances in the Minnesota state high school football tournament.

## Six Reasons to Run the Veer

Through experience, we have discovered the following advantages to the split-back veer offense.

- We use fewer plays and even fewer blocking schemes. We use essentially the same blocking on 90 percent of our plays. We can master our technique, encounter fewer mental errors, and get more repetitions during practice sessions. We feel that aspect this is the real secret to good execution.
- The use of a limited number of blocking schemes and techniques makes it more difficult for defenses to key our attack.
- The running backs and receivers are interchangeable, which reduces the amount of coaching required and allows for more flexibility in making substitutions.
- The split-back veer stretches the defense and forces them to play very disciplined on both sides of the line. They must cover the three parts of the triple option to each side of our attack against all formations.
- We are using excellent pass formations since we have three receivers. Also, our two backs are in the split alignment.
- The straight-ahead nature of the offense forces our backs to become harder runners.

# Introduction

*Coach Foley is a quiet, behind-the-scenes guy, who is an offensive mastermind. Coach Thole, on the other hand, is a very tactical, witty head coach, who is a great motivator and an excellent leader. Together they formed a perfect combination to teach and motivate high school-aged kids.*

*Football has had a huge impact on my life. Coaches Thole, Foley, and the Stillwater staff were instrumental in instilling in me the understanding that it is more than a mere game. Rather, it is an experience that is accompanied by numerous lessons that should be carried over into adult life. Getting knocked down, then picking yourself up and getting after it again, facing adversity and setbacks, all the while being able to adjust and cope are but a few of the values I have taken with me. Thanks for everything!*

—Adam Runk '97 All-State, Media "Player of the Year" 1996
Iowa State University Cyclones, Defensive Back, 1997–2002

The major purpose of writing this text is to produce an exceptional book on option football, while serving as a template and guide for coaches and players at all levels. Although defensive football played a major role in all of the successes we've enjoyed over the years, this book does not offer a detailed dissertation on the defensive aspects of the game. Instead, the emphasis of the text is on option football in general, and on the split-back twin-veer offense in particular. The book also details the mindset and philosophy that made this offense successful. Because the following pages are co-authored, the text occasionally features two distinctive writing styles that are meant to enhance, rather than to deter from, its overall readability.

The book provides a wealth of information for educators, laymen, spectators, and parents alike. Offering a mix of terminology specific to the complexities of the game and combined with language familiar to the layman, the book presents a concise, but understandable, account of a highly successful football program that has totally dominated the high school gridiron programs in the state of Minnesota over a span of three decades.

A brief history of the events and happenings that paved the way for the Stillwater area high school football program to emerge from one of obscurity to that of a power that was perennially ranked in the state's top 10 is included in the text. From the 1973 through the 1999 seasons, the Stillwater Ponies captured four large-school state championships and were silver medalists twice, while making a record setting 18 appearances in the Minnesota state high school football tournament. Over the span of 26 seasons, the "Big Red" won 13 conference championships and 12 section championships, and averaged an incredible 9.2 wins per season.

The ensuing chapters are multifaceted, covering a wide range of material pertinent not only to the game of football, but to the field of education and life in general. The age-old question of whether competition presents a healthy atmosphere or creates a negative environment for young people is discussed from both an educator's point of view, as well as a parent's. Competition and competitive spirit exist at every age level and in all walks of life. How to nurture and direct that competitive spirit is critical to the positive development of all youngsters.

The role that parents play with regard to their being involved in the educational and extracurricular activities of their children is also addressed. The book provides suggestions that are designed to guide parents and guardians in determining just how much involvement by them is too much. Unfortunately, some parents attempt to live vicariously through their offspring. As lifelong educators with a combined 70 years of experience in the classroom, we are well aware that positive reinforcement from parents and family is essential to successful learning. Parental involvement in the form of support, guidance, and encouragement is vital in nurturing existing potential in young learners.

The text also features suggestions concerning how to build a viable coaching staff at the high school level, and more importantly, keeping it intact over a long period. Continuity of staff is an invaluable asset, lending balance and stability to the program. Tips on developing motivational skills, along with effective incentive programs that enable players to raise their performance to a higher level of efficiency, are presented.

The little "nuances," the necessary ingredients in the art and skills involved in teaching and coaching young people, are also detailed in the book. Furthermore, techniques that worked well for us, and those that did not and were discarded, are addressed.

The heart and soul of this book, however, is an examination of option football in general, and the split-back twin-veer offense in particular. Stillwater High School developed its version of the veer attack in 1973. Over the years, slight adjustments in the offense have been made to stay abreast of the inevitable defenses being devised to stop it. Basically, the offense has remained constant since that time, with only minor "tweaking" to ensure that we were in step with the changing times.

In an effort to include the entire community of the St. Croix Valley, the offense was dubbed the Bayport veer in honor of Stillwater's closest neighbor, as well as part of the school district. Since its inception, dozens of high schools have had their gridiron coaching staffs observe and study the workings of this offense. Articles praising and analyzing the Bayport veer have appeared with regularity in state and national publications. Head Stillwater coach, George Thole, one of the more sought-out clinicians in the five-state area, annually speaks at a number of major football clinics, along with several smaller clinics, where he extols the many advantages of the veer offense.

Detailed descriptions and concise diagrams accompany a play-by-play scenario of the entire offensive package, along with key coaching points. Blocking rules, numbering systems, timing, and the intricate footwork involved are spelled out in precise sequence and detail. Basic alignments, sets, and formations are discussed, along with an in-depth examination of the role that motion plays in the offensive scheme. A simple, but effective, audible or check-off system is introduced, along with a very consistent, productive "two-minute" or hurry-up attack.

Fear of failure is an all-too-common factor that often leads to low self-esteem. In turn, such a low level of self-esteem results in subpar performances. Overcoming this fear of failing is a step in the right direction when developing a winning attitude. Positive self-images and high expectations, combined with continual reinforcement, are important aspects when creating a winning formula. Mindset and mental toughness can be developed to a degree, where they play a major role in the equation of success. A "winner" will never lose sight of victory and will treat a loss as merely a temporary setback. Mediocrity should not be a word in a coach's vocabulary. Anything short of all-out effort, enthusiasm, hustle, and total involvement by players and staff alike is unacceptable.

The path to success is steep and difficult to conquer. While getting to the "top" can be a major battle, staying there is even tougher. A fine line separates success from failure. The winning formula demands continuous attention from everyone involved—coaching staff and players alike—to establish and maintain a winning tradition. A successful program can crash and burn in a single season if attention is not paid to the minute inner workings of a team's essential systems. Complacency, apathy, or resting on a team's laurels are certain to reduce a successful program to one of mediocrity. Staying abreast and keeping up to date on any and all changes in the game, along with careful analysis of data from past seasons, are critical factors in the maintenance of a successful program. Attention to detail, both during the season and in the off-season, is required to sustain success, along with a strong work ethic and dedication by the entire staff.

Hopefully, this book will provide football coaches at all competitive levels with a tool that they can utilize to enhance the success of their programs. If it does, then the time and effort to write this book will have been well worth it.

—J.F.
—G.T.

# Prologue:
# Competition for Whom?

*The Ponies break the huddle and hustle to the line of scrimmage. This will be the final play of the game. Quarterback Justin Hesse sets his team, barks out signals . . . gets the snap from center and takes a knee as the clock ticks off the waning seconds . . . Five . . . Four . . . Three . . . Two . . . One. The game is over, and the Stillwater faithful rush onto the field to celebrate with their conquering heroes. The Ponies have done it again, winning their fourth large-school state football championship. The players, coaches, parents, and fans are delirious with excitement.*

The thrill of victory and the agony of defeat are at opposite ends of the emotional spectrum. Anyone involved in any form of competition has experienced both. Obviously, the first far outranks the latter for pure enjoyment and satisfaction. Webster's Dictionary defines competition as: "1. The act of competing: rivalry between opponents 2. A contest or match of competitors."

Kids love competing in any and all activities. In early childhood, the mere act of getting in line single file is a competitive experience for them. They elbow and push, attempting to be first in line. Observe a group of five or six youngsters skipping rope in an unstructured setting. If you were to get out a stopwatch and say to them, "I am going to count how many times you can skip rope successfully in a 15-second period … ready, go," every child, athletic or not, will do their best to see how many jumps they can get. Minutes later, they are eager to be timed again to see if they have improved.

Kids thrive in any event and when put to the test with a stopwatch. They revel in the sheer excitement of healthy competition. They want to know what the score is during a contest and how they are performing. Keeping score during a "numbers" basketball game in a physical education class is not demeaning to the participants, but rather, it contributes to the overall excitement of this large group activity.

Physical education is an integral part of academia, and as such, has its own set of standards, goals, and expectations. Participation, effort, attitude, and performance constitute the criteria used in measuring a student's progress. As is true in any other area of study, it will produce an often skewed and diversified learning curve. In the classroom, students are tested, graded, and evaluated on their performance and rate of overall achievement. Progress reports are handed out, and honor-roll lists are posted, available for public scrutiny, and often published in the local newspaper. Young people are subjected to competition early and often, and they learn to cope and deal with it as best they can. The rungs of the ladder to success are many and must be climbed one by one. Although encouragement, help, and support are necessities in guiding an individual, no one is going to pull or push you to the top. A person should seize any and all opportunities and remain focused while staying the course.

The behavior of kids does seem to have a childlike innocence when reacting to the score of a game or its outcome. They are able to take winning or losing in stride and are perfectly happy to move on to their next activity. By contrast, inappropriate or improper adult influence on this attitude can have a negative effect upon their overall thinking.

Like it or not, the real world is one of constant competition, whether it be on the floor of the stock exchange, in a court of law, the operating room, the classroom, or any of the diversified work places that we may be involved in as adults. Somewhere along the line, we must nurture that competitive spirit, keeping it alive in our young people, while channeling it into a positive experience for each and every individual.

## Winning and Losing

Vince Lombardi is often credited with the quote that, "Winning isn't everything, it's the only thing." The pros and cons of this statement have been the subject of endless debate. While winning isn't everything, its importance in the competitive world certainly should not be underestimated. Consider the lawyer in the courtroom or the surgeon in the emergency room, where finishing in the runner-up position is unacceptable. A person seeking advice regarding a pending lawsuit definitely wants to know the track record of the attorney defending him. Given the choice, he will select the lawyer that has the highest ratio of success in a court of law. A patient requiring intricate surgery to replace a heart valve wants the best possible surgeon to perform the operation. The successful attorney and surgeon enter their respective arenas highly motivated and filled with the knowledge necessary to accomplish the task at hand. They exude complete confidence in their ability to succeed, while blocking self-doubt from their thought process. For them, failure is not an option.

Obviously, even the most successful lawyer does not win every case he tries, nor does the most sought-after doctor save every patient in his charge. They do, however, approach each case with the confidence necessary to perform their duties to the very best of their ability. Focused individuals are mentally and physical prepared and will do everything in their power to be successful in each endeavor.

The successful classroom teacher and athletic coach follow the same approach in working with the young people in their charge. It is their duty to give their students and players every opportunity to enjoy the fruits of success. Instilling a mindset in students that challenges them to strive toward higher grades in the classroom is a goal of high priority and should be pursued relentlessly. By contrast, striving to win on the athletic field deserves the same critical attention given to the world of academics. In both cases, emphasis is placed upon getting the participant to perform at optimum proficiency.

Unlike the surgeon or the lawyer, however, where performance or lack thereof may mean the difference between life and death, such is not the case in the athletic arena. One must keep things in perspective and not lose sight of the fact that it is, after all, a game. Winning is fun, definitely outranks losing, and should be a goal when entering every contest. Losing has its lessons, but should be viewed as a temporary setback. Regroup, reload, make corrections, and get prepared for the next opponent.

High school athletic programs are one of the last bastions of discipline and accountability for young people moving through their teenage years. Our schools have been forced to cut back or condense many areas of student involvement. Physical education classes that once were required through the sophomore year are now electives even at the ninth grade level in many schools. Other junior high school students may only have physical education every other day. Grade inflation is becoming commonplace in many areas of academia. At a time when the bar has been lowered in so many areas of our society, it is refreshing to step into the arena, the gymnasium, onto the court or the playing field, and witness youngsters responding to the challenges that face them in this competitive world. The lessons taught and learned in cocurricular activities carry on long after the participant has finished his career. They are hard-earned lessons that stay with you for a lifetime and prove beneficial throughout your adult life.

## Parental Involvement

Educators are well aware that students are more likely to have success in the classroom when they come from homes where parents are actively involved in their children's school work. Parents should play a supportive role and be there to assist and reinforce learning.

Memo on the refrigerator door:
Johnny: Little League practice, 5 p.m.
Alice: Dance class, junior high, 7 p.m.
Scott: Soccer game, municipal field, 6 p.m.
Mom: Don't forget PTA, 7:30 p.m.

Sound familiar? Throughout the United States, this scene repeats itself daily in just about every home where young families are being raised. The schedules are busy and can be hectic. Being involved in their children's extracurricular activities generally is a necessity, not an option, for modern-day parents as they struggle with the question of just how involved they should be. A fine line separates genuine support for an activity and overindulgence by parents.

In the past, the time of year dictated the extracurricular activities youngsters were involved in. Seasons did not overlap with one sport season running into the next as they do at present. Year-round sports and traveling teams were unheard of and nonexistent. Young aspirants were not forced to choose or specialize at an early age, but were free to experiment with a wide variety of athletic experiences. Opting to be involved in one seasonal sport over another, such as basketball or hockey, did not become a necessity until reaching the high school level of competition. Because soccer was nonexistent on the American sports scene back then, football was the choice by the majority of young athletes during the fall season.

Kids walked or rode bicycles to and from neighborhood playgrounds or parks where they engaged in a wide variety of activities, some supervised and some not. Many of these were of the "pick-up" variety, choosing sides and playing with whatever numbers were available. In most cases, they had no umpires, referees, or parents for that matter, just kids improvising, adapting, and making the best of the situation. It wasn't unusual that whoever owned the football was the captain and was able to set many of the rules. The game often ended when the owner of the football had to go home for whatever reason. Frequently, neighborhood streets became the ball diamond, football field, hockey rink, or whatever the activity required.

Due to the vast difference in the ages of the kids involved, a definite "pecking order" developed at the playground. The older kids got the "big rink" and the better playing areas that were marked and lined for play, while the younger ones, biding their time, made do with lesser areas. In due time, they had the opportunity to "move up" in the hierarchy of things. Crosstown neighborhood traditions spawned at an early age, handed down by older peers and siblings, and the natural rivalries continued on into the high school years. A certainty of this bygone time is that if parents were looking for their kids, they knew exactly where to find them. They were at the local playground, the hub of activity for the majority of young people.

Because these activities occurred during the daytime hours, while mom and dad were at work or taking care of the house, parental involvement was at a minimum. Rides to and from play areas were not necessary because all were within walking distance. In fact, school buses were literally unheard of in the inner city areas because the schools were all neighborhood schools, making buses unnecessary. Youth coaches would tell their charges to be at a given area at a given time. Support from parents consisted mainly of making available to their children the tools of the trade like bats and balls, baseball gloves, footballs, and such, while encouraging them to be involved. Parental involvement as spectators in their children's sporting events came later as their youngsters moved into their high school years.

In today's hectic, fast-paced society, scheduling and distances to athletic facilities often dictate the necessity of parents being more than casually involved in their children's activities. They drive them to and from arenas, ballparks, and soccer fields, and often remain to observe practices or games. Once nonexistent, costs and athletic fees have soared during the past years. Over an extended period, this equates to parents having a substantial investment in both time and money in youth programs.

Care must be taken by parents to not become overly involved. Encouragement, support, and guidance are the key elements of their involvement. It should be kept in mind that recreation, fun, and enjoyment are the basic fundamentals of youth activities and amateur athletics. Undue pressure and insisting that a youngster play a particular sport or a particular position will generally lead to failure and total turnoff. It is important to nurture and develop the love of competition and sport that will stimulate the young person and bring their talents to full bloom.

## Why Football?

Football is the consummate team sport involving 22 players, 11 on offense and 11 on defense. Each position requires the execution of precise assignments that ultimately determine the success or failure for the entire team. Each play, whether on offense or defense, dictates a specific responsibility for every member of the team. Any one of the 11 team members not carrying out or accomplishing his assignment will ultimately lead to undesirable results. The game is as unique as the young men who play it and the people who fill the stadiums to watch it.

Further discussion of the interdependence and reliance of one teammate upon another can be cited by examining the game's most dynamic position, that of the quarterback. Quarterbacks are rated and judged on their leadership abilities along with their success in moving the football and putting points on the scoreboard. Passing percentages and numbers also play a major role in predicting the probability of success for the quarterback. The quarterback who is consistently lacking in these qualities will in all probability be replaced or encouraged to try his fortunes at a different position.

While the successful quarterback basks in the limelight, enjoying high numbers in the passing game and total offense, he is well aware of the intricate roles that his fellow teammates have played in his success. Aggressive blocking by his linemen allows him to operate along the line of scrimmage to successfully run the option game, along with providing protection for him in the passing game. The quarterback's job is much easier when gaping holes appear in the defensive front for his backs to run through. The onus of having to constantly make the big play is thus removed from his shoulders and is then shared by his teammates.

By contrast, dropped balls and poor routes by receivers, along with breakdowns in pass protection up front, quickly spell disaster for the quarterback and his mates. Inadequate blocking playside or backside by the offensive line equates into a stagnant and inconsistent ground game. Inept performances of the running backs only contribute to his growing problems. To be successful in his role as quarterback, he must depend upon the fulfillment of the responsibilities of all of his teammates.

Unlike other team sports, where a single individual may dominate and take over an entire game, football requires everyone to be on the same page at the same moment. For example, the hot goaltender in hockey, the overpowering pitcher in baseball, or the sharpshooter in basketball can almost single-handedly determine the outcome of a contest.

Incentives abound to entice young boys in opting to participate in the game of football. Football, by being a game of numbers, requires many players simply to round out a team roster. High schools and small colleges generally suit up everyone that is out for the squad, while other team sports like hockey, basketball, and soccer are forced to cut players from their rosters to get down to team size.

Opportunities for playing time in the sport of football are many. The young man who likes contact and is a hitter probably will find a place to play. Combined with special teams, kickoff, kick-return, punt, punt-return, extra-point, and field-goal along with 11 offensive and 11 defensive positions to fill, young hopefuls have numerous chances to be on the field come game time. Football is a seasonal sport and is not played year-round except at the highest levels, thus freeing up the athlete to be involved in other sports and activities.

It is not necessary for the youngster to begin playing the game at an early age as is true in many team sports. Hockey, baseball, basketball, and soccer require early training and development, and it is not unheardof for their participants to be more than casually involved as early as age five or six. If a young boy who hasn't been involved in organized football decides as a ninth or tenth grader that he wants to be on his high school team, there is a good chance that there will be a place for him on the roster. Some players in the professional ranks did not play high school football, but began their playing careers in college.

Of course, lifelong lessons are learned in the sport of football that can be carried into adult life. Teamwork, interdependence, and reliance on teammates cannot be overemphasized. By its very nature, football is the type of competition that develops future leaders in all areas of adult life, and it is safe to state that it more often produces the shepherds of the world rather than its sheep.

Jim Brown, the former Cleveland Brown's Hall of Fame running back and arguably one of the toughest men to play the game, when asked why he chose a career in professional football rather than a career in basketball, baseball, or boxing (many experts believed he could have been a serious contender to unseat then heavyweight champion, Floyd Patterson), stated simply, "The game of football is a total test of a man's very being, thoroughly testing his courage, strength, integrity, and overall character." Anyone who has played the game of football is well aware of the intensity and resolve in the locker room just prior to taking the field for the opening kickoff. It is an inner feeling that is hard to duplicate. It is an atmosphere in which one can hear a pin drop, and that results in the bonding of wills, inspiring a group of young men to perform together not as individuals, but as a single unit with a united purpose.

Whatever level of play—Little League, high school, college, or beyond—the strategies of the game range from simple to very complex. The ultimate goal of advancing the ball over the opponent's goal line is accomplished in a variety of ways. In a modern-day setting, these strategies range from full-house backfields, to twin backs, one-back sets, no-back sets, and from power football to run-and-gun, fast-break football. The game is mixed with grinding running attacks and all-out aerial assaults. Teams may line up toe to toe or spread out all over the field. The alignments, sets, and formations used pit offensive-minded people against one another, trying to outwit their counterparts on the defensive side of the ball. The strategies involved are unending and all-encompassing.

The co-authors, having enjoyed more than a modicum of success as players in high school and college, are in total agreement that the game of football at the high school level is very special. As players, many of our fondest memories date back to the teen years of involvement in the sport. Teammates then were the guys you grew up with, the same ones you played capture the flag, kick the can, and Little League with. They were neighborhood friends who attended the same grade school and hung out together at the local playground. They developed special bonds, accompanied by lifelong friendships. At the high school reunion, after meeting and greeting former classmates, they have a tendency to gravitate toward one another, reliving some of those memorable gridiron moments of days gone by.

Football, at any level, is an intense and electrifying game for spectators and participants alike. It is small wonder that the sidelines at Little League parks and high school stadiums are filled with enthusiastic supporters and fans. Whether it is a four-on-four, a pick-up game, the local high school team, the state colleges, or the pros, football reigns supreme as America's ultimate team game for the masses.

# 1

# Coaching 101

Untold numbers of books have been written on the subject of coaching football and other areas of athletics. All of these books are undoubtedly informative, and they range from very detailed accounts of coaching techniques to very basic books of instructions intended for the layman or the beginning coach. It is our purpose here to impart to the reader some thoughts on the qualities and talents necessary to attain success in coaching, not only the game of football, but other sports as well. For the purposes of this book, the terms "teaching" and "coaching" are synonymous; they are treated as such in the following paragraphs and are interchangeable.

## Leadership

It is our observation that the best and most successful coaches are also the outstanding teachers in the classroom as well. They are motivated, goal-oriented people, who set high standards for themselves and have great expectations of the athletes in their charge. Organization and efficiency are cornerstones in their approach to achieving intended outcomes. Motivation, along with methods used in delivering their product, is of the utmost importance in attaining any degree of success in the classroom or on the athletic field.

As a football staff, we have participated in and have attended numerous coaching clinics throughout the years. We attend, on the average, 8 to 10 clinics a year. From our experience, it is evident that the vast majority of coaches involved in high school football are competent and well-schooled in the game. To a man, they are capable of explaining and defending their offensive and defensive packages to their colleagues and constituents. Given the chalkboard or the overhead projector, most are adroit in presenting an understandable presentation on how the game is played. All of these coaches have a sufficient degree of knowledge of the X's and O's involved in coaching the game and are very enthusiastic about what they are doing. Something, then, separates the highly successful coach, who is consistently in the winner's circle, from the vast majority of his peers, who are more often bridesmaids than brides.

# Pedagogy

The dictionary defines a pedagogue as "a teacher or a schoolmaster," and pedagogy as the "art of teaching or the profession of teaching." Note the phrase: "art of teaching." Sound teaching techniques demand particular skills. The most successful instructors are gifted people who are able to reach out and project their ideas and concepts to a group of learners with vastly different learning abilities.

Though armed with a wealth of knowledge, combined with superior vocabulary skills in their respective fields, the effective teacher/coach does not attempt to dazzle or impress his charges with his overall knowledge of subject matter. Rather, he is flexible and resourceful enough to break down the material so that it is understandable to the majority of the learners. Although essential to success, it is not an easy skill to master.

A lesson taught is not necessarily a lesson learned. You cannot assume that because the lesson or skill has been presented that it is understood and grasped by all of the students. High school players need constant instruction and continuous coaching. Repetition, drill, and review are necessary tools to reinforce learning and to ensure that the skills being taught will be retained. This approach is highly evident on the football practice field, where daily drills constantly bolster and reinforce learned responses. Teaching and learning are ongoing activities and must not be allowed to become stagnant.

Educational reforms have run rampant over the past several decades. Witness the rise and fall of programs such as modular scheduling, outcome-based education, year-round school, and profiles of learning, to name a few. It often seems as though the people farthest from the classroom or playing field have the most input on how educational and extracurricular programs should be run. They sit in their mahogany foxholes, far behind the field of battle, and make dynamic decisions that ultimately affect the entire educational system. Generally speaking, the most successful instructors are the career-type teachers and coaches who are in it for the long haul, not those who teach and coach for a few years and then leave the classroom to become educational consultants or the like.

# $E = mc^2$

In the early 1900s, the noted physicist Albert Einstein created a whole new way of thinking by making known to the world his now famous equation explaining the theory of relativity. Suddenly, man was asked to view mass and energy as one and the same, but with different manifestations, a concept difficult for the average mind to conceive. In modern jargon, it is referred to as "thinking outside the box."

Obviously, to begin to understand Einstein's theory, you would have to possess a solid background in the physical and chemical make-up of the cosmos. Basic calculus helps to lay the groundwork in grasping the concept of relativity. To reach the plateau of total understanding of these ideas, a specific developmental program, including a scope and sequence of related math and science courses, is necessary over a period of time. The developmental program must include the teaching and reinforcement of the basic concepts of mathematics and scientific principles, so as to lay down a workable foundation.

The teaching techniques that go on in the classroom have a correlation to the instruction that takes place on the athletic field. The word "teaching" is a verb with a connotation that implies action, thus dictating to the teacher to be active, rather than passive, in his presentations.

If an instructor were able to recruit only top students to take a class in relativity or quantum analysis, the actual teaching of said class would be a relatively simple task, for obvious reasons. Because it is unrealistic to be in such a utopian setting in public education, the task confronting the teacher becomes one that will demand his most tried-and-true methods of reaching out to all of the students, not just the top performers. The ensuing paragraphs cite some of the tools that successful and resourceful teachers and coaches bring to the educational table.

# Preparedness

Keep in mind the simple but dynamic age-old motto of the Boy Scouts of America: "Be prepared." As old as this motto is, it has gone unchallenged through the many decades it has been in place. It is a given that the good teacher must have a solid background in the subject matter that is to be presented. His understanding of the concepts that are being taught should be thorough and complete. Anything less is unacceptable. A lot of truth is to be found in the adage: "By failing to prepare, you are preparing to fail."

Assuming the teacher/coach has a sound foundation in the subject matter gained from graduate and undergraduate studies, workshops, and clinics, his presentation and delivery of the material becomes of the utmost importance to the learner. Learning should be an enjoyable and exciting experience, and it falls to the instructor to create an environment that is conducive to both. How a coach creates such an environment is directly proportionate to his success.

Preparedness on the football field equates to being equipped to handle and deal with any and all situations that may arise. By expecting the unexpected, the successful coach is arming himself with the tools needed to adapt to, and cope with, any sudden or unforeseen changes that often occur. Teams that are well coached have been drilled and taught to react quickly and automatically to such events.

In our football program, no possibility is ignored, and we practice situations such as what to expect and how to react if the game goes into overtime. We make it a point to continuously review and explain the subtleties of the rules governing the game. For example, our punt-return men are always schooled to be alert for the "first touching" rule during a punt by our opponent. Not infrequently, members of the punt-coverage team may simply down the ball and then jog off before the official has blown the ball dead. Being alert to this situation gives us opportunities to scoop the ball and advance it with no risk of a turnover. Because offenses must be able to attack goal-line defenses, "goal-line-crunch" drills are an integral part of our weekly practice schedule. We make it a point to practice both our running attack and passing attack in the red zone. Our practice plan dictates that we execute our offense under game situations such as first-down plays, second-and-long, third-and-short, and so forth. No part of the game is so small and unimportant that it can be ignored.

## Salesmanship

It can be said that the teacher/coach who enjoys consistent success in the classroom or on the athletic field, while some of his colleagues may struggle just to get through the day, is simply a better salesman than his counterparts. Being able to sell yourself and your ideas is no small task. Successful educators and coaches are by nature excellent salespeople who are astute in marketing their product. Gaining the confidence of the intended learners is a vital step in the learning process. Players and students, believing that they have the best possible coaches/teachers at their disposal, will perform at a much higher level of efficiency. Total belief in yourself and your program, combined with what you are attempting to accomplish, is a must in ensuring desired results. Once you have gained their attention and have won their respect, learning will follow.

In the private sector, top salespeople are constantly rewarded with additional perks along with their large commissions. Incentives and final results play a major role in selling your product, whether it is merchandise, ideas, concepts, or programs.

# Enthusiasm

Enthusiasm may be defined as "being inspired, or possessing a strong warmth of feeling, combined with keen interest and fervor." You can readily add words like excitement, tenacity, elation, ardor, élan, and so on. They all add up to being excited about your programs and ideas. If you aren't excited about what you are doing, you cannot expect your pupils or players to be excited. Teachers and coaches can ill afford to have a bad day in the classroom or on the athletic field because a subpar performance equates to short-changing the young people involved in their programs. For teachers, the curtain goes up on a new group of expectant learners every 60 minutes, five times a day. Enthusiasm is contagious and is quickly picked up by those around you. Everyone is capable of being excited and of exuding enthusiasm. Don't be passive when executing your presentation. Turn up the jets, and make every teachable moment count.

# Motivation

The great motivators of the world are also the great success stories of the world. Motivational skills are discussed elsewhere in this text, so at this point, suffice it to say that motivation is one of the great intangibles of the teaching/coaching profession. The ability to get "into" a young person's head, to get them to perform beyond the conscious level, is a major hurdle to conquer in attaining successful results.

Numerous methods are used in motivating teams and individuals, most of which are spontaneous rather than learned, which is not to say that motivational skills cannot be learned and developed, but that the most effective techniques are often inborn. By nature, some people are just great motivators.

However you choose to motivate, it is important to be yourself. Not everyone is a George Patton or a Vince Lombardi. What works well for one individual may not work well for the next person. Trying to emulate someone or something you are not is a sham and is easily identified by students or players. Being sincere, honest, and fair in your approach to educating your charges is a step in the right direction. Through experimentation early in his career, the teacher/coach is able to determine those motivational techniques that have been most effective for him.

# High Standards and Great Expectations

The educator who sets high standards and lofty goals for himself and for those in his class or on his team is much more likely to experience success than a counterpart who is negligent in this area. The philosophy that "Life is tough, but I am tougher" can be ingrained in your players. Goal setting and planning are necessary tools in any game plan. Careful analysis is especially critical in the formulation of realistic and attainable goals. Daily, weekly, and seasonal planning is of the utmost importance to the coach and teacher alike. These plans and goals may be altered and adapted to fit your needs as dictated by the personnel available to you, along with changing times, budgets, and programs.

Having high expectations involves raising the bar for all participants in the program. Care must be taken to include every member of the team when critiquing the squad. Reserve players should feel that they play an important role in the overall scheme of things. In short, treat them all as equals, and treat them as you would like to be treated.

Never use inexperience or youth as an excuse for subpar performances. Players are "green" or inexperienced only if you allow them to be that way. Under the direction of the coach, team members should be included in developing team and individual goals. These should be realistic and attainable goals, but never compromised or watered down. If players can be convinced that they are capable of attaining the seemingly "unattainable," a major step toward the winner's circle has been taken. Expectations falling short of this mental set most likely will result in performances that are subpar and bordering on mediocrity. The role of the coach, then, is to challenge his players to reach beyond the conscious level of attainment, while moving on to a higher level of achievement. It is healthy to think big. Players should be taught to "seize the moment," and to take advantage of opportunities when they arise. A wise sage once noted that, "Opportunities are really never lost, because someone will always be there to take the ones you missed."

The expectations put upon our offensive units are lofty. Every play in our playbook is designed to score a touchdown, provided of course that each member of the offensive unit carries out and executes his assignment. The basic philosophy of our staff and our players is to view every possession as a scoring opportunity, and we expect to score every time we have the football. We frequently practice our offense from the 20-yard line, insisting that our ballcarriers sprint to the end zone on every play. Points on the scoreboard is the only valid statistic that counts when evaluating the impact of your offense. Yards gained and first downs made are meaningless if the offense comes up empty.

The United States Marine Corps believes that military victories are made possible for two reasons, one being what they call "esprit de corps," and the second being unflagging discipline. They also contend that the latter is a direct product of the former.

## Common Sense

The person responsible for creating the acronym KISS ("Keep it simple, stupid") has made a major contribution to the field of education as well as to the coaching fraternity.

Care should be taken not to overcoach an individual. If desired results are obtained, even though the player's style is unorthodox, it may not be necessary to change the performer's technique. Witness the sprinter who consistently runs the 40-yard dash in 4.4 seconds, but has a less-than-picture-perfect starting stance. Attempts should be made to improve his stance and starting techniques; however, if significant improvement in performance does not result, it is permissible to allow the runner to revert to his former, more comfortable stance. Consider the high school quarterback who can throw the ball from point A to point B with consistency, but does not have picture-perfect delivery. It is a moot point for the coach to spend all kinds of time trying to change his release. As long as he continues to complete a high percentage of his passes in practices and games, the coach is able to move on to develop other skills that will lead to overall improvement in his performance as a quarterback. For example, it may free up some time to work with him on making simple reads in the secondary while improving his ability to identify man coverage versus zone coverage. In the world of fine arts, it is commonly extolled that "form follows function." The oft-repeated phrase, "If it ain't broke, don't fix it," applies here as well.

Football, the ultimate team game and arguably the most complex of all team sports, certainly is not in the realm of rocket science. Granted, with 22 offensive and defensive positions along with special teams, combined with the numerous sets, plays, and formations, the case for complexity can certainly be made. The coach should be leery of adding to the complexity of the game by employing needless jargon that may be confusing to the players, while adding difficulty to the task of teaching them. The use of terminology such as "head-up," "outside shoulder," "inside shade," "slant technique," and "blast technique," to mention a few, are descriptive terms and easily understood. The intent here is not to diminish the intricacies involved in coaching the game of football, but rather to suggest additional and alternative methods to employ in teaching the game to young players.

Modern-day football coaching staffs have rapidly grown in numbers over the years. Staff numbers may be anywhere from a dozen to as many as 20 or more at the high end of the scale. Often, the number of coaches involved is directly proportionate to the complexity of the program being offered. The more coaches you have, the more responsibilities can be and are assigned to the various position coaches. It follows that each coach is eager to add his expertise to the mix. The key is to find some common ground so that the best skills of each individual coach can be put to good, practical use.

In the fall of 1975, we had a varsity staff that consisted of only three coaches. We feel that we were as effective as a staff then as we were in later years when we enjoyed a coaching staff of eight full-time coaches. By necessity, we shared the duties of coaching all phases of the game. Obviously, it was necessary to take a simpler approach to coaching the game back in the 1970s. With only three coaches involved, we certainly did not have time to overcoach any phase of the game. We kept our playbooks brief on both sides of the ball. We made simple reads on offense and defense, while keeping our terminology as basic and understandable as possible.

No matter how many offensive formations and defensive sets you have, the name of the game is still blocking and tackling. The team that is able to do these two things with the greatest consistency is the team that is going to win most of the time. On offense, it is absolutely necessary to establish early on at least one phase of your attack that you are able to "hang your hat on." With the game on the line, you do what you do best. For us, when push comes to shove, we know that the outside veer, the base play of our offense, is the solution. We know it, and our players know it. Defensively, it boils down to playing team defense, making reads, gang tackling, and pursuing relentlessly to the ball.

## Assessing Personnel

Undoubtedly, one of the most significant skills of the coach who enjoys continuous success is his ability to assess the talent of players available to them. This talent becomes of particular importance in the game of football because of the many positions to be dealt with, along with special teams and the like. It is one of the more underrated skills and is too often taken for granted. At the high school level of play, where you have such a diverse talent pool to select from, it is no small task evaluating the strengths and weaknesses of the individual players. Making the correct moves and decisions at this stage will go a long way in dictating the outcome of the season. Placing players in a position where they have the greatest opportunity to obtain success will bode well for the entire team. Our credo is that every boy who comes out for football and wears the red and black on Friday nights is capable of making a contribution to the team. No contribution is deemed too small. It may be as a special-teams player or a scout-team player, or whatever. Getting players into the right positions, while at the same time making them feel positive about themselves, is a key to assembling a winning attitude and a winning combination.

It is equally important to instruct coaches at the junior high level to be patient and tolerant, particularly with the large, gawky kid who has not yet grown into his body. All too often, the quick, agile seventh- or eighth-grader gets most of the attention and the majority of playing time, while the gangly, not yet coordinated youngster either sits on the bench or becomes discouraged and drops out of the program. Never give up on or write off the young player at this age level who seems too clumsy or too slow to contribute. He may mature into the franchise-type player that every coach is looking for.

The dedicated junior high school coach can be an invaluable asset for any high school football program. The "career-type" coach at this level is often a rare commodity.

Too often, they coach for a couple of years after their hiring, and upon reaching tenure, have a tendency to drop out of coaching, but retain their teaching contract. The key is to hire enthusiastic young coaches who are eager to be lifetime coaches, either at this level or higher. Once they are established, it is necessary to make them feel that they are an important part of the overall picture by including them in the workings and successes of the program. The astute head coach of any high school football program makes it a point to both recognize and reward not only the coaches on his immediate staff, but also those young men working and coaching at the junior high school level. These coaches/mentors make football an enjoyable experience, while at the same time keeping young boys interested in and excited about the game.

## Skilled Versus Unskilled

Whatever the sport—football, hockey, basketball, soccer, or baseball—varying degrees of skill level are involved in each. The successful coach, along with his staff, will take care of business by seeing to it that they spend ample time every day working on individual and team skills pertinent to their sport. In the game of hockey, skating ability being a given, the primary skills involve the players' adeptness in handling the puck. It includes an individual's skill in basically three broad areas: shooting the puck, passing the puck, and the ever-important stick-handling techniques. While these obvious skills need constant attention in daily drills, they are but a part of the overall workings of the game of hockey. Statistics bear out that, on the average, a high school hockey player taking a regular shift over a three-period game actually handles the puck less than a minute in a forty-five minute contest. This statistic equates to the individual playing more than 98 percent of the game without the puck. In striving for success, it then behooves the coach to spend adequate time developing the unskilled aspects of the game such as positional play and checking angles, along with just being in the right place at the right time.

Not many high school football teams are blessed with highly skilled athletes to line up at the majority of positions. The blue-collar approach for any prep coach dictates that he and his staff concentrate on the aspects of the game they are able to control. Many high school coaching staffs spend a great amount of their practice time working on the skilled areas of the game and have a tendency to ignore or downplay the vast area of the game that basically involves unskilled behavior. These include critical aspects of simple things such as proper alignment on offense, defense, and special teams. Good footwork, timing, stances, and quick feet by linemen and backs alike are developed during daily "team-takeoff" drills. Disciplined play, along with the concept of "team," is critical to the success of any program. The framework of any good team has a solid foundation supported by the intangibles of attitude, hustle, enthusiasm, and great expectations. Every squad member, from first to last, is capable of developing these vital areas, thus allowing them to contribute to the overall success of the program.

# Age Has Its Privileges

Stillwater High School has been a senior-oriented football program for the past three decades. Seniors dominate the starting line-ups on offense, defense, and on special teams. Our players know that if they have been faithful to the program and have worked in the weight room, having paid their dues so to speak, they will be given every opportunity to be in the lineup somewhere on Friday night. If a senior and a junior are equal in ability at a given position, the senior will get the nod as the starter. It is then up to him to keep his position. Seniors who lack the ability to be everyday players are given every chance to make their mark on any one of the many special teams. Emphasis on the importance of being on a special team is a daily ritual at our practice sessions. Players take pride in being on as many "specials" as possible. It is not unusual that a senior player is honored with the prestigious title of "special-teams captain" for the entire season. In short, our program thrives on senior leadership.

This approach has enabled us to play anywhere from 55 to 90 players per game, either on scrimmage plays, special-teams play, or both. Even in games that are very close and are decided by a single touchdown or an extra point, we will have gotten 50 to 55 players into the game. The more players you can get to be active "shareholders" in your program, the greater the chances you have for overall success.

The philosophy of involving as many players as possible on game nights has paid off large dividends for us over the long haul. In many instances, our senior-dominated lineup was able to establish a tradition of taking control of the game in the early going. In turn, this afforded our younger players the opportunity to gain valuable game time playing experience.

When we are able to sub down by units both offensively and defensively, our expectations of the reserves remain the same as with the starters. We expect the offense to move the football and the defense to stop the opponents. Junior players and non-starters thus attain veteran status early in the season.

# Community Involvement

Any athletic program can be enhanced by the involvement and the cooperation of the community at large. The extent of involvement should be governed and regulated under the auspices and direction of the head coach along with the local school district. Civic and fraternal groups such as the Rotary, Lions, and the V.F.W. are often available to lend support, while maintaining a low profile. Local businesses and restaurants displaying posters, schedules, and athletic calendars add interest and support, while newspaper and media coverage affords further exposure of the program and all of the athletes involved.

Our youth football program is conducted and run by an all-volunteer group of men. Hundreds of young boys, grade 4 through grade 6, are introduced to the game at an early age. Youngsters are fully equipped and are placed on teams according to their grade level, size, and elementary school area. Many former football players return to the program to coach and officiate each year.

# Leave 'Em Laughing

It is not unusual for many in the education/coaching profession to take themselves too seriously. After all, it is a very serious business. A good sense of humor is an invaluable asset for one to possess in any field of endeavor, but is of particular value to those working with the young people of our society. You must always keep in mind that the program is for the kids; the kids are not for the program. It is best if you are able to laugh at yourself on occasion. A good sense of humor in the classroom or on the athletic field can be as valuable a trait as knowledge of the subject matter. When properly mixed, they combine to form a recipe that is invaluable to the instructor. The old adage, "You can catch more flies with honey than with vinegar," is aptly put. Learners always perform better in an environment that is relaxed and comfortable for them, as opposed to the environment that is tense and strained. Players and students should look forward with anticipation and excitement to being a part of your program. Dread or apathy are the alternatives, and ultimately lead to undesirable results.

Our practice sessions are always run in a businesslike manner, tempered with varying degrees of intensity and urgency. Taking care of business does not have to be an "in your face" proposition. You do what you have to do to ensure that your team has every opportunity to be successful on game night. Players are never dismissed and sent home on a negative note. When they leave school for the evening, we want them to have positive thoughts and feelings about their team and teammates. Sometimes,

Figure 1-1. Practicing offense

it is necessary to "bring them up" after a session that didn't go particularly well. A positive self-image is optimal on the road to achievement.

To ease the players' tension and pre-game butterflies, consider telling a joke just prior to leaving the locker room and heading to the field for the opening kickoff. It can help relax the squad and allow them to see their coach from a different perspective. It can also put things in perspective: It is a game, not a life or death situation. "Go out and do your best, and don't sweat the rest!"

# Game Plan Formulation

When preparing for the next opponent on our schedule, we as a staff are more concerned with what we are doing and how we are doing it, rather than with the doings of the other team. Our thinking being that by controlling the things we are able to control, while executing our attack both offensively and defensively, we are then masters of our own destiny.

It should not be inferred that we are neglectful of, or take lightly, the strengths and tendencies of our opponents. By contrast, we operate under the credo, "Respect all opponents, but fear none." Formulating a sound game plan entails input from the entire coaching staff. Careful analysis of the latest scouting reports, along with notes accumulated and filed from previous encounters, are examined and studied at length. The availability of a multitude of game films affords the coaching staff a vast sea of information on the innermost workings of our opponent.

When assembling the offensive game plan, we concern ourselves with specific criteria pertaining to our opponents, knowing that defensively they absolutely have no way that they could align themselves to take away our entire attack. The rationale of our offensive philosophy was "to scratch where it itches," or attack where they are most vulnerable.

The first and foremost concern is identifying the opponent's basic defensive front and the alignment of their linebackers and secondary, along with coverage tendencies. We have to determine if they remain in their base defense the majority of the game, or if they alternate defensive fronts frequently. It is important to know if they camouflage their coverage, and if so how, along with tendencies of man coverage compared to zone coverage and such.

A careful examination of opposing personnel reveal who the "stud ducks" are, along with any glaring weaknesses in their defensive alignment. Questions regarding personnel to be answered include: Do they flip-flop any personnel—if so, when and where? Do they favor the wideside of the field? Who is their strongest defensive back, and is he assigned to cover the best receiver? Who is their best linebacker, and what are his tendencies? Who is their most active and versatile down lineman? What and where, if any, are their weaknesses on defense? Do they have an Achilles heel that we can exploit?

A critical look at defensive tendencies is of particular importance in formulating the game plan. Again, questions to be answered include: Do they blitz often or illustrate a pattern of blitzing on a particular down? Do they tip their hand when they blitz? Are they predictable in given situations such as on first downs or in long-yardage situations? What is their goal-line defense, along with their tendencies in putting it to use? How do they react and respond to motion?

Scott Ertle, Stillwater Gazette

When preparing for the next opponent on our schedule, we as a staff are more concerned with what we are doing and how we are doing it, rather than with the doings of the other team.

Upon analyzing the data and information amassed from scouting reports, notes, and game films, we formulate our offensive game plan for our next opponent. Noting their strengths, weaknesses, and tendencies, we zero in on the areas we feel confident that we can attack successfully. As offensive coaches, we do not alter or change anything in our attack when preparing for the new opponent. Through the years, our offense has been modified and streamlined so that needless adjustments are unnecessary. Rather, we concentrate on the execution of our attack, while pinpointing specific plays we feel the opponent will have difficulty defending. Thus, the majority of our practice time during the week is spent honing and sharpening our offense with added emphasis in the areas we know we will be able to exploit.

In formulating the offensive game plan, it behooves the coaching staff to scout their own attack to determine if they are showing any tendencies and are therefore predictable. Careful dissection of game film of the offense, along with play selection, readily reveals whether or not we as a team fall into a specific pattern in given situations. This is a critical area of preparation and is often overlooked by coaching staffs.

Sometimes, the best-laid plans may fall apart and completely collapse moments after the kickoff. An injury to a key player or some other unpredictable occurrence may change the intended course of the game. In the 1984 state championship game, our starting quarterback went down on the third play of the game and had to watch the remainder of the contest on crutches from the sidelines. This situation forced us to "tweak and temper" our plan of attack. Care must be taken so as to not abandon the original game plan because of such an unforeseen happening. Patience is necessary, particularly early in the game, and it may be necessary to punt the football during the first couple of possessions. The punt is an offensive play and is used in the ongoing battle of field position.

The coaching staff that is well prepared will always have an alternate plan ready to go if plan A fails. Inclement weather, rain, snow, or high winds may dictate a shift in emphasis in attacking the opponent. By expecting the unexpected, coaches will be in position to make sideline adjustments quickly and smoothly, with little or no interruption in the flow of the game. Always make sure that all of your key backup players get plenty of repetitions each day in practice.

Finally, when formulating the offensive game plan, exercise caution so as to not to attempt to do too much. Know the opponent's defensive strengths and weaknesses, along with their tendencies. Stay the course, and offensively do the things that you do best. Do not make wholesale changes in your attack to compensate for the opponent's defensive scheme.

# 2

# A Typical Week

Our practice sessions are always very well organized. Practice begins sharply at 3:20 p.m. each afternoon with all participants expected to be on time. Unexcused absences, being late to practice or to a meeting, are unacceptable. Practice sessions are intense and businesslike, but at the same time, relaxed so as to create an atmosphere that does not result in driving anyone away. The game of football is tough enough, so making a practice session into a boot-camp situation is counterproductive to the overall success of the program. Positive reinforcement from the coaching staff is a staple commodity in daily interaction with players. Policy dictates that we never send a young man home having negative feelings about himself, his teammates, or the program.

## Day-by-Day Practice Routines

Each position coach has a syllabus for the day's workout, including time slots for calisthenics and agility, individual techniques, specialties, team scheme, along with plans covering offensive and defensive emphasis. Copies of the day's workout are posted at the entrance to the locker room and are considered required reading for all players. An ironclad rule employed in our practice sessions is that we never move from one area of concentration to another until the coaching staff is satisfied that we are ready to move on. While chalk talks are a part of our weekly preparations, the football field is always our preferred chalkboard, affording the players a more realistic view of proper alignment, along with greater understanding of their assignments and techniques necessary to carry them out.

The following is a brief look at the organization and implementation of activities involved in a typical week. Keep in mind that this outline is flexible, subject to subtle adjustments per week as dictated by variables such as weather conditions, the upcoming opponent, along with particular emphasis on any given phase of our game plan.

Standard operating procedures for every practice session include team-led stretching and calisthenics under the direction of the team captains, but closely scrutinized by the coaching staff. It affords quality time for the staff to mingle with and interact with squad members in a relaxed atmosphere. On completion of calisthenics and stretching, players sprint to their position coaches for work on individual skills, including quickness, agility, and ball drills.

A real plus factor in our individual period is that it is carried out under the leadership of the players themselves. During the first two or three days of two-a-day practices, position coaches install individual drills that are specific to their areas of concern. Once players establish proper sequence and technique and execute to the satisfaction of the position coach, the coach turns the responsibilities over to them. This procedure entails leadership involvement by every member of the squad, and the players take pride in the responsibilities bestowed on them.

## Monday

Monday evenings are game nights for our junior varsity team. We do not refer to them as the J.V. or junior varsity, because it assigns a negative label to certain members of our total team. Instead, we call them our "Broncos." We take great pride in our Broncos, and make it very desirable to be privileged enough to suit up and play for them on game nights. Typically, 95 to 98 percent of our varsity starters are products of our Bronco teams. Our entire varsity coaching staff attends the Bronco games, either as coaches on the sideline or as evaluators in the stands or press box. The results of the game, individual performances, and team performances are discussed and brought to light the following day at practice.

Because we only have about 30 to 35 players at practice on Bronco days, we get a great deal accomplished with our starters and the players who will get the majority of playing time on Friday night. After team calisthenics and stretching, we go into a short agility period and then get immediately into our team scheme. Defensive emphasis comes first with our starting defense facing the plays they had to defend against on game night. Half of the practice time is spent on defense. When our defensive coordinator is satisfied that they have had sufficient looks at the opposing offense, we then move to offensive emphasis. Because we have our best players present from the offense and the defense, as well as the fact that we are able to get so many quality repetitions, we accomplish a great deal on Monday nights, or "Bronco Nights."

## Tuesday

The entire squad practices on Tuesdays. After a quick recap of the Bronco game from the previous night, highlighted by comments from the coaching staff, we settle down to work. Tuesday practices are open-ended, meaning we would stay longer than usual. Parents are familiar with this routine and adjust their schedules accordingly.

After calisthenics, stretching, and agility drills, we have an individual period. Offensive and defensive linemen go with their respective coaches for intensive individual technique work. During this period, which lasts for 20 to 25 minutes, the remainder of the squad comes together for our Tuesday ritual of option-drill day. For this entire time slot, the running backs, quarterbacks, tight ends, and wide receivers run our complete option package against the defensive ends, linebackers, and defensive secondary. The drill is done at game speed and is live, except for tackling. Every third or fourth play is a pass play, thus forcing the defenders to read and react, and at the same time, it sharpens our passing attack.

The option drill does wonders for our option game, as it affords us the luxury of numerous repetitions against a live perimeter, giving us a variety of reads. Our backs improve their timing and execution while our wide receivers hone their blocking and receiving skills. Defensive ends, linebackers, and defensive backs have to react to the game-like scene before them. All players are constantly rotated in and out of the drill, giving us total participation.

The individual period is followed by our team scheme period. We always begin with defensive emphasis and do not move to offensive emphasis until we are satisfied that our defense has covered all its bases. Offensive emphasis follows and continues until we feel that we are hitting on all cylinders. We finish practice with conditioning and then head for the film room to view footage of our upcoming opponent.

## Wednesday

Wednesday is designated as kicking game day. After cal, stretching, and agility drills, we forego the individual period and move directly into our kicking game. We like to do this during mid-week because we are in full pads and are live, except for tackling. The order of events is always the same, beginning with our kickoff, then proceeding to our kick-return, followed by our punt team, and finally our punt return. We never move from one discipline to the next until the coaching staff is completely satisfied with the performance of said team. We also attempt field goals from various angles and distances and finish up this period with our extra-point team.

After the kicking game, we moved immediately into team scheme with both defensive and offensive emphasis rounding out the remainder of our time on the practice field. After practice, it is back to the film room to look at more footage of our opponent if we deem it necessary. Our players are prepared to stay late.

## Thursday

Thursday is designated as special teams day and is conducted in shorts, helmets, and shoulder pads. Practice begins with the players sprinting through the goalposts onto the field for our pre-game warm-up. From the warm-up, we go directly to our kicking game, following the same order as in Wednesday's practice. Our goal is to move crisply through the kicking game, reviewing assignments and polishing our execution. When satisfied, we move on to our two-minute drill, which pits the starting offense against the Bronco defense. The ball is spotted on our own 20-yard line and the parameters are given to the quarterback: down-and-distance, time remaining on the clock, and how many time-outs he has left. Our defensive coaches spot the ball, keep time, and otherwise officiate the game situation. Our audible system, clock management, and overall performance under fire are easily evaluated during the two-minute drill. We always make sure our key backup players are also involved.

Our goal is to move through our entire practice quickly, but thoroughly, and get our players off their feet and off the practice field as soon as possible. Thursday is always an exciting day, not only because it is the day before game day, but it is also "spaghetti-dinner day." The kids look forward to it, as do the coaches, managers, and parents. It presents a relaxed atmosphere, allowing the players, coaches, and parents to mix and socialize in an unstructured setting. The parents of the juniors and seniors sponsor and serve the dinner, while clean-up is the responsibility of the squad members. Our final words to them are: "Take your helmets home, clean and polish them, get your game face on, and get a good night's sleep. Visualize yourself performing at peak proficiency. Eat the right foods this evening and at school tomorrow: this means no junk food."

## Friday

Game day! All players (no exceptions) wear their game jerseys to school. The rule of the day is: "Go home immediately after school, get off your feet, relax, and eat a decent pre-game meal. Everyone come dressed in full game attire (carry helmet and shoulder pads), and be in the weight room at least 25 minutes before departure time. Relax, listen to the music, and visualize yourself performing at your top level." After a pre-game talk from the head coach, which includes last-minute instructions and answering any questions players may have, we load the buses and depart for the stadium.

Post-game: everyone gathers in the locker room or weight room for a brief recap and evaluation of that night's game. We set a curfew for the night that is agreeable to all. Upon dismissing the players, the coaching staff and spouses (or favorite others), along with a few close friends, gather at a local "watering hole" for a late night snack.

Win or lose, sleep is always an elusive commodity following a big game. It is an opportunity to kick back, relax, and savor the moment, while unwinding from the adrenalin high of the previous 24 hours. Some of our more successful thoughts and innovations are spawned at these informal gatherings.

## Saturday

On Saturday, our entire coaching staff meets sharply at 8:00 a.m. in the film room at the high school to break down film from the previous night's game. Offensive and defensive staffs work in separate rooms to do their analysis and then come together for a total assessment and evaluation of our overall performance before the arrival of the entire squad. The Saturday morning practice fulfills several major areas of concern:

- We are able to assess and take care of any injuries that we were unaware of from the previous night.
- Rather than waiting the entire weekend, we are able to bring the whole squad and staff together without delay (which is particularly important in regrouping after a loss).
- It enables us to take care of game assessments, scouting reports, and game films, hand out game awards, and feed the squad following a victory.

The players, dressed in shorts, helmets, and shoulder pads, have to be on the practice field at 10:00 a.m. After a very brief period of stretching and agility drills, the team comes together to listen to the coaching staff's comments and evaluation of the previous night's performance. It is followed by a scouting report on the following week's opponent. The staff members who scouted the team the previous night conduct the report. Written scouting reports are handed out to all players after practice.

By 11:00 a.m., the entire team gathers in the film room to view the previous night's game. The whole group is brought together to bolster unity and team cohesiveness. One coach narrates the entire film, while position coaches offer advice and constructive criticism where needed.

If we were victorious the previous night, the entire squad enjoys a pizza lunch before they leave for the weekend. An award ceremony is held (only for victories) and players are awarded stars, skulls, and splatter decals for touchdowns, sacks, interceptions, touchdown blocks, and so forth. The players are dismissed for the rest of the weekend by approximately 1:00 p.m.

## Sunday

Our varsity coaching staff meets at 7:00 p.m. on Sundays at the high school to prepare for the next opponent. This meeting involves viewing footage of their previous games, assessing their strengths and weaknesses, and formulating a workable game plan. Generally, the offensive and defensive staffs work separately, then join forces to tie everything together. We strive to be finished by no later than 9:30 p.m.

As stated previously, this overview has been a brief look at a typical workweek in our football program. Things vary from week to week, depending on a variety of factors, but this outline is an accurate picture of what goes on each week throughout the season. Our approach is tried and true, has been tested by fire over the years, and has been proven successful over a span of more than three decades.

*Note*: On any given practice day, if the head coach along with his staff feels that progress was such that they are satisfied that the team is ready and that as a squad, they are precisely where the coaches want them, he will call them together, letting them know he and the coaches are pleased with their progress, and then he will send them in early. Besides being a great morale booster, it contributes additional incentives for energetic and enthusiastic practice sessions. The players work hard while anticipating the chance to get through a practice session a little earlier than scheduled.

Scott Ertle, Stillwater Gazette

Positive reinforcement from the coaching staff is a staple commodity in daily interaction with players.

# PLAYBOOK

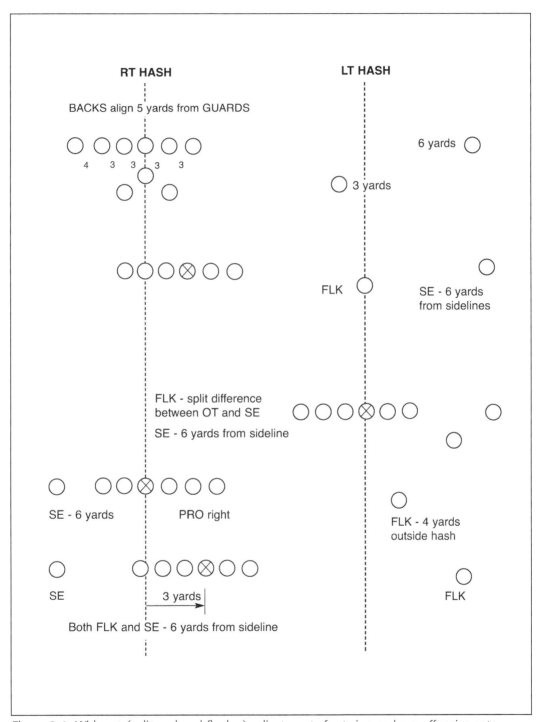

Figure 2-1. Wideout (split end and flanker) adjustments for twins and pro offensive sets.

# Hard Dive

The hard dive is considered the base play of the offense. To be successful, the offensive line must create running lanes by getting movement on the defense, thus allowing the back to "run to daylight." We tell our players that we must get at least three yards per play.

## Assignments

*QB*: Opens back with near foot, crosses over, reaches back on the third step, and hands the ball off one-and-a-half yards behind the line of scrimmage.
*DB*: Landmark is the inside hip of his tackle; shoulders square as he meshes with the quarterback and "runs to daylight."
*PB*: Sprints for the sidelines, simulating pitch relationship with the quarterback.
*SE*: Crossfield technique
*FLK*: Crossfield technique
*C:* Over, playside gap
*ONG*: Blocks 1, zone technique, outside breast. *Note*: If 1 is a linebacker, takes zone step and reads the defensive tackle's charge.
*ONT*: Blocks 2, zone technique; blocks through inside breast, but locks on if he slants.
*OFF G:* Blocks 1 through playside gap, scoops; replaces the feet of the center.
*OFF T:* Blocks 2 through playside gap, scoops.
*TE*: Blocks 3 on the inside number. Uses drive technique and gets movement off the line of scrimmage in any direction.

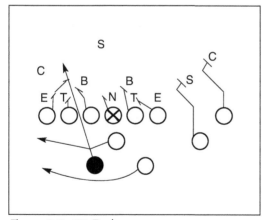

Figure 2-2. 52 Eagle

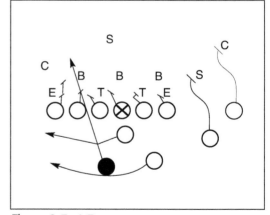

Figure 2-3. 4-3

# Dive Option

This play looks like the hard dive, but it is a predetermined keep or pitch. It is a two-way option between the quarterback and the pitchback.

## Assignments

*QB*: Open steps, using second step as a balance step; steps back on third step and reaches for the defensive back; reads the first man who shows after the dive fake.
*DB*: Drives for the inside hip of your tackle, makes a great fake, and blocks pursuit.
*PB*: Sprints for the sidelines, looking for the pitch. Maintains five-yard pitch ratio.
*FL*: Slow blocks pitch support.
*SE*: Slow blocks deep third.
*C*: Over, playside gap
*ONG*: Blocks 1; zone blocks through outside breast.
*ONT*: Blocks 2; zone blocks through outside breast.
*OFF G*: Blocks 1 through playside gap; scoops and replaces the feet of the center.
*OFF T*: Blocks 2 through playside gap; scoops.
*TE*: Releases flat across the face of the defensive end and blocks pitch support.

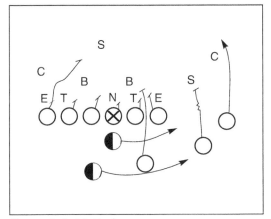

Figure 2-4. 52 Eagle

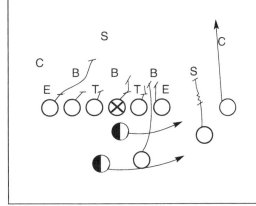

Figure 2-5. 4-3

# Counter Dive

This quick-hitting, inside misdirection play will create just enough counter movement on the defense to set the blocks; not a good goal-line play.

## Assignments

*QB*: Executes counter footwork; hands the ball off as deeply as possible, and then carries out a fake.
*DB*: Takes a short jab step with the inside foot, hits the landmark of the center-guard gap, and "runs to daylight."
*PB*: Waggle steps in opposite direction; sprints for the sidelines, simulating pitch relationship with the quarterback.
*FL*: Quick technique
*SE*: Quick technique
*C:* Over, near linebacker, zone technique.
*ONG*: Blocks 1, zone technique.
*ONT*: Blocks 2, zone technique.
*OFF G*: Blocks 1, zone technique.
*OFF T*: Blocks 2, zone technique.
*TE*: Takes double-team step toward defensive tackle with his near foot, explodes downfield on the second step, and blocks downfield on the middle safety.

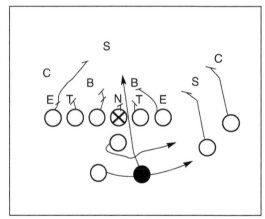

Figure 2-6. 52 Eagle

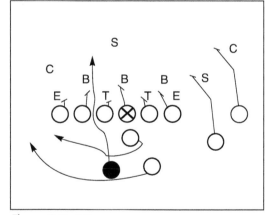

Figure 2-7. 4-3

# Counter Option

This play freezes the linebackers and puts stress on the perimeter.

## Assignments

*QB*: Executes his counter technique, passing the ball in front of the diveback's pouch. Continues to the end man, attacking his inside shoulder, and keeps or pitches. Must be ready to pitch quickly due to hand-changing end man.
*DB*: Takes counter dive path, rolls over the fake, and blocks pursuit.
*PB*: Sprints for the sideline, looking for the pitch.
*FL*: Onside, slow blocks pitch support, offside crossfield technique.
*SE*: Onside, slow blocks deep third, offside crossfield technique.
*C:* Over, playside gap
*ONG*: Blocks 1, outside breast; zone-blocking scheme.
*ONT*: Blocks 2, outside breast; zone-blocking scheme. Note: If 2 is the end man on the line of scrimmage, pulls and blocks the linebacker in the immediate area.
*OFF G*: Blocks 1 through playside gap; scoops.
*OFF T*: Blocks 2 through playside gap; scoops.
*TE*: Releases flat across the face of the defensive end and executes an arc block on the defender responsible for the pitch. Landmark is the outside breast.

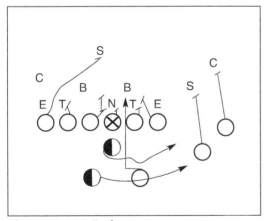

Figure 2-8. 52 Eagle

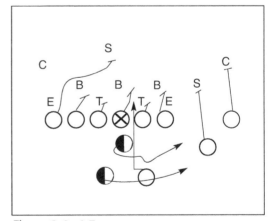

Figure 2-9. 4-3

# Outside Veer

The outside veer is a true triple option, which attacks one hole wider than the hard dive. The quarterback must read the defensive end to determine give or keep. This call is a great one when you're inside an opponent's 10-yard line.

## Assignments

*QB*: Steps down the line, meshing with the diveback on the third step. Reads the defensive end and reacts accordingly. If in doubt, he hands it off
*DB*: Drives for landmark of outside hip of his tackle. Squares the shoulders at the line of scrimmage; runs for daylight or makes a great fake.
*PB*: Sprints for sidelines, looking for the pitch.
*FLK*: Crossfield technique
*SE*: Crossfield technique
*C*: Over, playside gap
*ONG*: Blocks 1, zone technique, outside breast.
*ONT*: Blocks 2, zone technique, outside breast.
*OFF G*: Blocks 1 through playside gap; scoops. Replaces the feet of the center.
*OFF T*: Blocks 2 through playside gap; scoops.
*TE*: Blocks over; first inside, on or off the line of scrimmage; uses combo technique. If double-teamed, works butt toward tackle on contact.

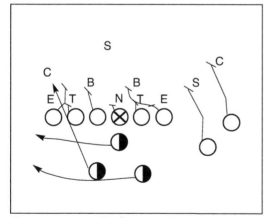

Figure 2-10. 52 Eagle

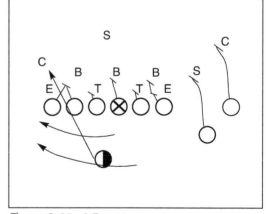

Figure 2-11. 4-3

# Slant or Cutback Dive

The cutback dive is a very effective play against teams that attempt to stop the option with quick flow from the inside. It is also effective versus split defenses. This play gives us great cutback action. This play sets up a whirley option.

## Assignments

*QB*: Knows the position of first down lineman and steps accordingly. Makes mesh as deep in the backfield as possible. Reads the guard's block versus Eagle defense.
*DB*: Aims at the first down lineman from the nose of the center to the on-guard. Always thinks cutback. Reads the guard's block versus Eagle defense.
*RB*: Two-step whirley action; stays in pitch phase. We also run a whirley option.
*FLK*: Blocks his man using inside-out technique.
*SE*: Blocks his man using inside-out technique.
*C*: Over, near linebacker
*ONG*: Blocks 1, zone technique.
*ONT*: Blocks 2, zone technique.
*OFF G*: Blocks 1 if linebacker; scoops if down lineman.
*OFF T*: Blocks 2, scoop technique.
*TE*: Blocks 3, inside breast.

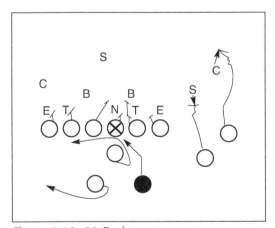

Figure 2-12. 52 Eagle

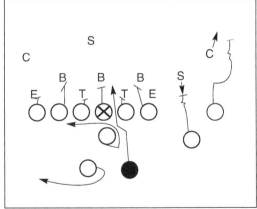

Figure 2-13. 4-3

# Lead Option

The option is a great change-up for defenses that get used to seeing only the triple option. This play is our version of a sweep.

## Assignments

*QB*: Drop steps, open step, attacks the end downhill.
*BLCKR*: Runs a tight arc course and blocks the man responsible for the pitch. Doesn't drift.
*BC*: Sprints for the sidelines, looking for the pitch. Follows lead blocker as if he left footprints in the snow.
*FLK*: Cracks first linebacker to his inside.
*SE*: Slow blocks deep third.
*C:* Over, playside gap
*ONG*: Blocks 1, zone through outside breast.
*ONT*: Blocks 2, zone outside breast.
*OFF G*: Blocks 1 through playside gap; scoops. Replaces the feet of the center.
*OFF T*: Blocks 2 through playside gap; scoops.
*TE*: Blocks first linebacker over/or to your inside.

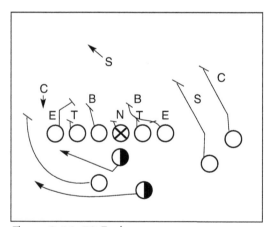

Figure 2-14. 52 Eagle

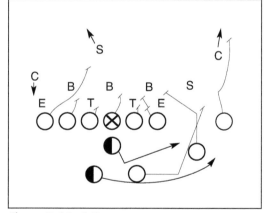

Figure 2-15. 4-3

# Short Trap

The short trap is the basic play of our misdirection series. The pitchback creates flow, which enables the off guard to trap the onside tackle. This play can be run to either the split or tight side of any formation versus most defenses.

## Assignments

*QB*: Drop steps, steps at a 45-degree angle and meshes with the offside back; continues with Pony option fake.

*BC*: Steps forward, and then drives for his landmark, the outside hip of onside guard. Runs to daylight.

*PB*: Sprints for sidelines opposite the hole and simulates pitch relationship with the quarterback.

*FLK*: Quick technique

*SE*: Quick technique

*C:* Over, backside, high-pressure control technique. Note: "Over" only refers to down lineman, one away or two away.

*ONG*: Blocks first down lineman from "nose" of center to his onside shoulder. Uses drive technique and gets movement. Blocks zero or one away.

*ONT*: If covered by a linebacker, combo inside. Blocks first linebacker inside.

*OFF G*: Pulls flat across the center's box and blocks first man past center; drive technique, numbers.

*OFF T*: Blocks 2, drive technique, inside number; cannot allow 2 to gain penetration; seals to center.

*TE*: Blocks 3 with drive technique; landmark is under chin; must get movement.

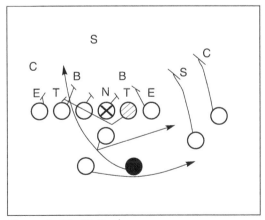
Figure 2-16. 52 Eagle

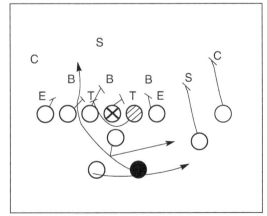
Figure 2-17. 4-3

# Pony Option

This play is the misdirection option coming off of the misdirection trap. The diveback will create flow away, which enables the off guard to pull and seal the onside linebacker. This play can be run either to the tight or split side of any formation.

## Assignments

*QB*: Drop steps, then steps back toward the diveback, extends arms; rides the diveback and then attacks inside shoulder of end man on the line of scrimmage.
*DB*: Drives for landmark, butt of the center; rolls over the fake and blocks pursuit.
*PB*: Counter, then sprints for sidelines, looking for the pitch.
*FLK*: Onside, slow blocks pitch support; offside, crossfield technique.
*SE*: Onside, slow blocks deep third; offside, crossfield technique.
*C:* Over, backside, high-pressure control technique. Note: "Over" only refers to down lineman.
*ONG*: Blocks first down lineman from "nose" of center to his onside shoulder. Uses drive technique and gets movement.
*ONT*: Blocks 2, controls outside breast.
*OFF G*: Blocks 1 through playside gap.
*OFF T*: Blocks 2, drive technique, inside number; cannot allow 2 to gain penetration.
*TE*: Takes flat lateral step inside to create misdirection. Pushes off inside foot and executes normal arc release. Blocks the defender responsible for the pitch; landmark is the outside breast. Plays away, blocks free safety.

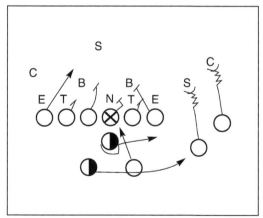

Figure 2-18. 52 Eagle

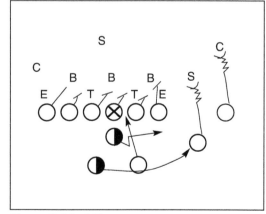

Figure 2-19. 4-3

# Rollout Passing

## Assignments

*QB*: Rolls with run-pass option.
*LB*: Blocks first man outside of tackle.
*PB*: Blocks second man past linebacker's block.
*FLK*: Pattern
*SE*: Pattern
*C*: Blocks zero; if zero goes backside, checks linebacker; if zero goes to cover, center goes backdoor.
*ONG*: Blocks 1; if 1 is a linebacker that goes to cover, helps out inside.
*ONT*: Blocks 2.
*OFF G*: Blocks 1.
*OFF T*: Blocks 2.
*TE*: Blocks 3 or pattern.

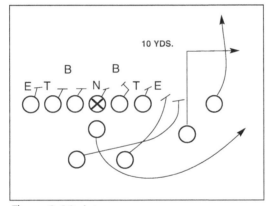

Figure 2-20. Jet

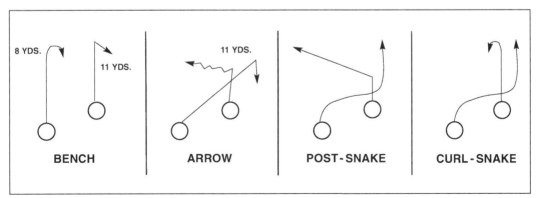

Figure 2-21. Combination pattern with twin receivers

# Play-Action Passing

## Assignments

*QB*: Executes triple option and drops to three-step.
*PB*: Runs option and should be ready to help tackle or block 4.
*DB*: Hits outside hip of guard and reads blitz.
*FLK*: Pattern
*SE*: Pattern
*C*: Man, off linebacker, backdoor
*ONG*: Blocks first down lineman.
*ONT*: Blocks second down lineman.
*OFF G*: Blocks 1, backdoor.
*OFF T*: Blocks 2.
*TE*: Blocks 3 or pattern.

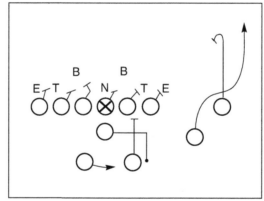

Figure 2-22. Curl, snake

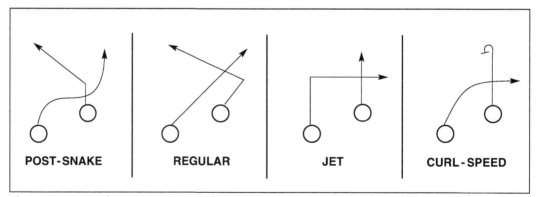

Figure 2-23. Combination pattern with twin receivers

# Double Dive Pass

## Assignments

*DB*: Linebackers
*FLK*: Streak
*SE*: Streak
*C:* Zero man
*ONG*: First down lineman
*ONT*: Second down lineman
*OFF G*: First down lineman
*OFF T*: Second down lineman
*TE*: Post

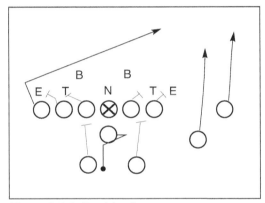

Figure 2-24. Double dive pass

# Dump Passes

## Assignments

*BG*: Option block
*BKT*: Option block
*C:* Option block
*ONG*: Option block
*ONT*: Option block
*TE*: Pass route or option block

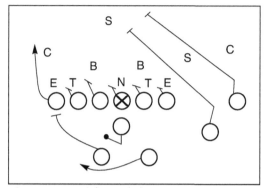

Figure 2-25. Tight end dump

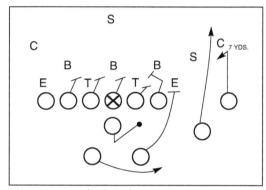

Figure 2-26. Flanker dump

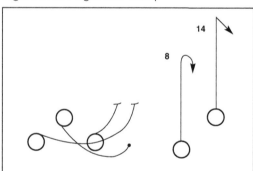

Figure 2-27. Roll, bench

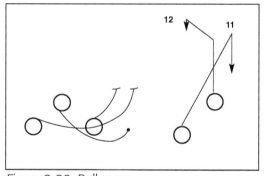

Figure 2-28. Roll, arrow

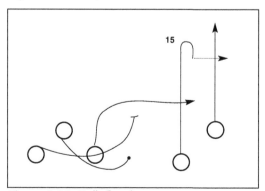

Figure 2-29. Roll, flood

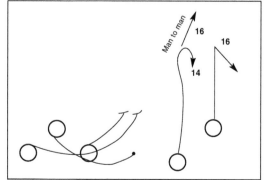

Figure 2-30. Roll, comeback

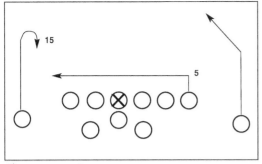

Figure 2-31. 3 pattern

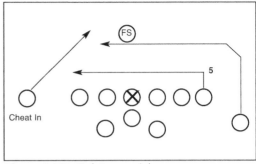

Figure 2-32. Safety special

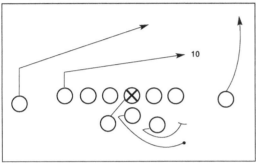

Figure 2-33. Bootleg

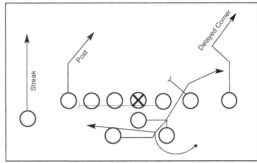

Figure 2-34. Waggle left pass

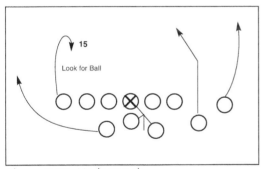

Figure 2-35. Understreak

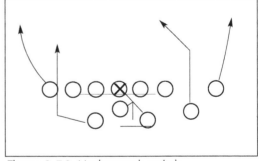

Figure 2-36. Understreak switch

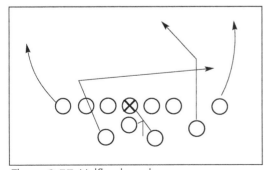

Figure 2-37. Halfback under

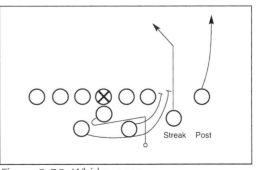

Figure 2-38. Whirley pass

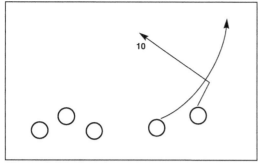

Figure 2-39. Regular

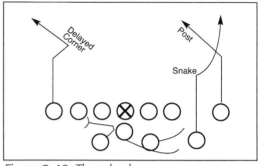

Figure 2-40. Throwback

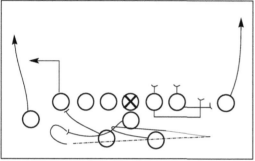

Figure 2-41. Roll, halfback screen

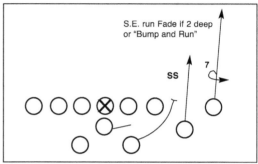

Figure 2-42. Flanker dump

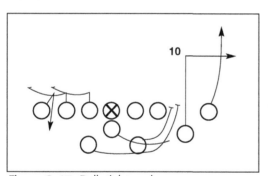

Figure 2-43. Roll, tight-end screen

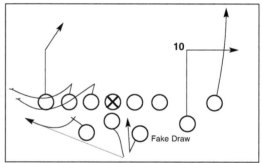

Figure 2-44. Draw, screen

# 3

# Training the Veer Quarterback

## Quarterback Routines

Our feeling is that we can take an athlete of average ability and teach him to read the option and run our offense successfully. When we are fortunate enough to have a really talented player at the helm, we are then able to exploit our opponents to the maximum.

It is our policy to see to it that the quarterback aspirants are rewarded for their diligence in learning and remaining at that position over a period of time. Obviously, all of our quarterbacks have been decent athletes or they wouldn't have lined up at quarterback, and in most cases, they were talented enough to be able to play at another position.

For the young man who is not the starting quarterback, the chances of his being on the field at game time are limited. To satisfy his competitive spirit, along with his desire for playing time, and to ensure that we always have a solid backup at quarterback, we play him at flanker back and wide receiver. He is in the game early and often, and is considered a "regular."

This philosophy delivers multiple benefits to our program. Not only do we ensure ourselves of a solid one-two punch at quarterback, we are able to utilize both athletes under game conditions to improve the total effectiveness in our attack. If the starting quarterback is injured, his backup is already "battle hardened" and quickly eased into the role of leading the team and guiding the offense. He is not forced to come off the bench "cold." It also proves to be a great morale factor because the athletes know from tradition that, as a coaching staff, we see to it that, having paid their dues, they will be in the game on Friday night.

## Stance

The necessity of the quarterback moving quickly along the line of scrimmage in option football mandates a proper and consistent stance. Height, body type, and athleticism will play a part in allowing for individual differences in his stance. We like our quarterback to "stand-tall" when receiving the snap from the center. The knees are comfortably bent with the feet parallel and approximately shoulder-width apart. Weight is equally distributed on the balls of the feet. His feet are never staggered so as not to tip off the intended direction of flow.

The stance is balanced and comfortable, allowing the quarterback to move with ease in all directions. All of the bending is done with the knees, the back straight—never "stooped," allowing him to mesh smoothly with the running backs. The quarterback's head is always on a "swivel," with his eyes fixed on the maneuvering defense in front of him. The stance and "body-language" of the quarterback sends a positive message that transmits poise, leadership, and confidence to his teammates.

## Receiving the Snap (Quarterback-Center Exchange)

Every play begins with the snap of the football, so its importance cannot be overstated. Games can be and are often lost by the bungled center-quarterback exchange.

Assuming a proper stance, the quarterback places his hands, wrist deep, under the butt of the center with his elbows slightly bent and close to the body. His thumbs are pressed together or may be overlapped; fingers are extended and comfortably spread with the index finger aligned in the middle of the center's butt, forming a good pocket to receive the football. We prefer to have his throwing hand on top, exerting enough pressure on the center's butt so that the center feels the quarterback's hands. If the centers are firing out on every play, the upward pressure of the quarterback's hands allows them to "move with the center," thus reducing the chance of a fumbled snap.

Quarterbacks familiarize themselves with all of the centers on the football team. Rotating centers and quarterbacks in daily ball drills allows the quarterback to be comfortable when receiving the snap from any of them. He has enough to think about at the line of scrimmage without concerning himself with how the ball was coming up to him. Due to the importance of the center-quarterback exchange, the center should snap the ball to the quarterbacks in all ball drills whenever possible. You do not want the center to snap the ball and be static; insist that he "fire out" with every snap of the football. This approach ensures that the quarterback's hands move with the center.

# Making the Handoff

Unlike many offensive schemes, a cardinal rule for our quarterbacks is: every handoff is made with both hands on the football. We never want a handoff with only one hand holding the ball. The quarterback moves quickly away from center, both hands on the ball, with the point of the football pulled in toward the belt buckle in what we call the "ready position." In making the handoff, the quarterback will extend his arms, delivering the ball into the pocket formed by the dive back. On "non-read" plays (dive, slant, trap, isolation), he will "look" the ball into the pocket, making certain it is properly seated.

At the exchange point, the quarterback's outside hand places the ball into the belly of the dive back, while the inside hand acts as a guide and then is smoothly removed. The quarterback should not "lunge" when making the handoff; rather, he must keep the ball and follow the dive back up the hole. Upon completion of the handoff, the quarterback continues down the line, carrying out his fakes. The option game relies on deception and execution, so we insist upon the carrying out of fakes by all of our backs on every play.

On all read plays (outside veer, split veer, and all options), the quarterback was trained to "feel or sense" the presence of the dive back at the mesh point, while keeping his eyes riveted on his read. It is important to note that when running the outside veer and the split veer, the quarterback would never seat the ball and then pull it out. Unlike other veer teams, dive backs were taught to "lock on to the ball" when they felt it placed in their pocket, even if it meant dragging the quarterback with them.

# Executing the Pitch

The option game dictates that the quarterback will be pitching the football frequently during the course of a game. It is imperative that he is able to pitch the ball equally well with either hand. A lot of time is spent each day with all of the quarterbacks working on proper techniques in pitching, both moving to their right and to their left.

The quarterbacks are paired off and introduced to the pitch with a stationary drill. The quarterback must assume a good athletic stance with the ball in the "ready position." When pitching to his right, he steps toward his partner with the right foot, while extending his right arm directly at the pitchback. In executing the pitch, he will rotate his wrist, thrusting the thumb downward while the little finger turns upward. His arm movement is not unlike that of a boxer throwing a punch (jab) at an opponent. When properly executed, it results in a soft, end-over-end pitch that is easy for the pitchback to handle. Ideally, the pitchback should receive the pitch at a height just above his belt line. A high pitch will "stand him up," and is difficult to catch. "Never pitch the ball in his face, and never pitch with two hands or under duress." This drill is done repeatedly to the left and to the right. When quarterbacks are not involved in any particular drill or function, they should be working on their pitching techniques. A quarterback never has any reason to be just standing idly; he always has a skill he can be working on.

Progression is made from the stationary pitch to a drill that has the quarterback pitching the ball while on the move. The drill is a three-step move, run both to the left and to the right. It involves an open step with the playside foot and a crossover step with the other foot to balance up. The third step is the pitch step and is taken in the direction of the pitchback. It is a good drill that does not take up a lot of space and can be done quickly if time is a factor.

In our offense, the running backs line up with their heels five yards from the line of scrimmage. They maintain this distance while staying in pitch phase with the quarterback. Before practice begins, the quarterbacks pair off to sharpen their skills in pitching the football. They align themselves on the five-yard chalk stripes and pitch the ball back and forth while running the width of the field. This drill is done over and back two times, affording them the opportunity to execute the pitch repeatedly, both to the left and to the right.

When making the pitch, the quarterback, if possible, must come under control with his weight balanced up. In a game situation, he will often get hit after making the pitch and must rock back and give with the blow.

## Throwing the Football

In any offense, from the wide-open spread formations to the more conservative looks of the wing-T or the wishbone attacks, the importance of the quarterback's skill in throwing the football cannot be overstated. Whether the game plan calls for passing 20 percent of the time or 60 percent of the time, a key success factor is the ratio of completions to attempts. Obviously, accuracy is critical in measuring the success or failure of the passing game. Along with arm strength, proper throwing technique of the quarterback involves a wide array of fundamental skills, including proper grip, footwork, hip rotation, and release. All of these related skills must be performed in a smooth and rhythmic manner to ensure consistency in the passing game.

Just as the pitcher warms his arm up gradually before throwing heat, it is important for the quarterback to take time to throw easily at first and slowly progress to the point where he is ready to put "something" on his throw. Daily warm-ups should include a variety of ball drills, allowing the quarterback ample time to properly loosen up, and at the same time affording him the opportunity to work on proper throwing motion and release.

# Grip

While most quarterbacks grip the ball differently, a number of constants should be followed when teaching a young player the proper method of gripping the football. Hand size, along with length of fingers, plays a role in dictating how each individual will grip the ball. Whatever the grip favored by the quarterback, it should be consistent.

The football is gripped only with the fingertips, maintaining a space between the ball and the palm of the hand. Placement of the fingers on the laces is arbitrary and there is no right way or wrong way to place them. Some quarterbacks prefer to spread their fingers farther apart, having their index finger well back toward the tip of the football, while others prefer to grip the ball more toward the middle with the fingers spread equally. Ease and comfort play a major role in finger placement on the ball.

When teaching quarterbacks to grip the football, start by having them place their pinky finger between the fourth and fifth laces, keeping their fingers equally spread so that the index finger lines up on the back stripe of the ball. The thumb aligns and immediately opposes the index finger, maintaining a space between the ball and the palm of the hand. Care must be taken to grip the ball firmly, but not too tightly.

Experimentation and subtle adjustments will be necessary when taking into account the inevitable individual differences that are bound to occur. In youth football, when dealing with players with smaller hands, the introduction of proper grip and throwing motion is best accomplished with a smaller, youth-sized football.

# Throwing Motion

Throwing motion will vary per individual, depending upon arm strength and other physical factors involved. Whereas some quarterbacks are capable of throwing deep with a lot of zip on the ball because of physical strength, others are forced to use more of their bodies in getting the ball down the field. Following are the basic steps for teaching quarterbacks proper throwing motion:

- The quarterback should start in a comfortable stance with the feet slightly more than shoulder-with apart and the front shoulder pointed toward the target.

- The quarterback should move the football into throwing position with the front hand, pushing it up by the earhole of the helmet like a baseball catcher preparing to throw to second base. The front hand is the guide hand.
- With the lead foot, the quarterback should step toward the target with the front elbow pointing at the intended receiver.
- He should rotate the hips while keeping the lead foot pointed at the target.
- He should push off the back foot, driving the lead elbow downward.
- Shifting the weight to the front foot, the quarterback should deliver the ball just over the head by rotating the wrist so that the ball comes off of the index finger.
- In the follow-through, the weight should be on the front foot, and the thumb of the throwing hand should be pointed toward the ground.

The previously mentioned steps are simply a guideline used in teaching a young quarterback the normal progression in his throwing motion. Each individual is different and should be dealt with accordingly. If the thrower is consistent in hitting his target a high percentage of the time, but has an unorthodox delivery, so be it. Spend more time working on some other phase of his game that needs improvement.

# Daily Quarterback Routines

Besides drills involving pitching the football, center exchanges, and normal warm-up drills, quarterbacks must follow a daily routine developed to further improve their skills in handling and throwing the football. These daily rituals were hardly unique to our program, but were drills gleaned from various clinics and programs. While these drills represent just a few of the many routines, if followed diligently, they will greatly enhance the performance of your quarterbacks.

*Ball Drop Drill*: Quarterbacks can do this drill anytime they might be idle. The purpose of the drill is to improve the grip on the football and general ballhandling skills. It helps strengthen the muscles of the hands while contributing to the overall dexterity of the quarterback. Simply stated, the quarterback grips the ball properly, with arm extended out from the body, then drops the ball and quickly re-grips it. This drill is done repeatedly with the right hand and then the left.

*Ball Around the Body*: Again, this drill can be done at any time on the field or at home in the backyard. It is intended to further develop the ballhandling skills of the quarterback. Standing with his legs slightly bent and feet about shoulder-width apart, he will pass the ball between his legs in a figure eight, both clockwise and counter clockwise. Variations include holding the ball in "ready position" just in front of the belt buckle, then passing the ball around the midsection in both directions.

*Knee Drill*: Quarterbacks pair off, facing each other five yards apart and down on one knee, with the opposite foot pointing at his partner (right knee down if right-handed, left knee if left-handed). The quarterback starts with the football at his sternum, pushes the ball into throwing position, and then with proper release and follow-through, throws to his partner who then does the same. They execute 10 repetitions from five yards, then separate to 10 yards and repeat. A variation of the drill is to have the quarterbacks do the same drill with the opposite knee down. Sometimes, under duress, quarterbacks are forced to throw off of the "wrong foot," and this drill simulates that action.

*Hip Rotation Drill*: Quarterbacks pair off five yards apart with their shoulders facing each other. Again, with the football at the sternum in both hands, he will push the ball into the throwing position and then deliver it to his partner, making sure to rotate the hips while releasing the ball accompanied by proper follow-through. They should do 10 repetitions, and then repeat the same drill from 10 yards.

# Passing and the Veer Attack

While the entire passing package is discussed in a separate chapter, this section will discuss the basic philosophy of the passing game and the quarterback's role in executing it. It is our firm belief that the ground game is instrumental in setting up the passing attack. Although labeled as a running, ball-possession-type team, the forward pass is an integral part of our overall offensive system. Our aerial arsenal affords five different series, allowing us to move the ball through the air. They include:

- Play-action series
- Sprint-out series
- Half-roll series
- Three-step series
- Down-the-line series

An exact and precise evaluation of the quarterback's throwing and running skills dictates which of these methods we emphasize and zero in on. Some quarterbacks will be able to execute the entire gamut of the passing attack, while others will be able to handle a limited portion of it. As coaches, we determine early on what his strengths and weaknesses are in the passing game and then isolate and concentrate on what he does best. Asking him to do what he was incapable of doing successfully is not unlike asking someone to take a nap on the railroad tracks; it ultimately ends up in disaster.

The play-action series and the sprint-out series have proven to be the foundation of our passing attack over the years. In certain seasons, they were the only series used in throwing the football. In both series, a limited number of routes are used in order to simplify the execution demands put on the quarterback. Upon analysis of the quarterback's skill in throwing the ball, three or four patterns from each of the two series are used that he would be able to complete with consistency. The play-action series is a priority because of its close correlation to the running attack. It is a quick-hitting series with short timing routes.

With a particularly strong runner at quarterback, emphasis is placed on the sprint-out series to put additional pressure on the perimeter, forcing the defense to play both the pass and the run. It is a safe method of getting the ball to the outside in the hands of a good athlete with the option to run or pass. In the event that a team is blessed with a pinpoint passer at quarterback, a team is able to exploit the entire passing package. This package includes the half roll, which is a version of the drop back, along with the three-step or quick game. The entire passing attack is discussed at length in a separate chapter.

# Reading the Outside Veer

Along with the called dive, the outside veer is the base play of the offense. Being a true triple option, it puts tremendous pressure on the defense, who are forced to defend the dive, the quarterback keep, and the pitch to the outside. It is a fast-hitting play that can only be run to the tight-end side of the formation. Timing and execution are of the utmost importance to the success of the play, thus demanding continued repetition in daily practices.

The equipment used when working on timing and execution is a commercially purchased item that is unrolled and stretched on the ground. On it are marked the alignment of the offensive linemen along with their respective line splits. The splits of the interior linemen are constant and never varying. Three-feet splits separate the center and guards and also the guards and the tackles. The normal split for the tight end is four feet, but he may widen his split in given situations. He will never allow a linebacker to "stack" on him.

Our running backs line up with heels five yards from the line of scrimmage, so veer drills are set up along the five-yard stripes on the field. The landmark of the dive back on the outside veer is the outside hip of the playside tackle. He will run a 100-yard dash directly at his landmark with his eyes fixed on the point of attack. The quarterback opens with the playside foot, with the football in the "ready position" and pointed directly at the hole, and a sprint down the line of scrimmage toward the mesh point. He will mesh with the dive back between his third and fourth steps. However, he must make his decision to hand off or keep the football in his first two steps. He hugs the line of scrimmage and must never bow back. The timing of the outside veer dictates that the quarterback does not throttle down at the mesh point.

For the quarterback directing an option attack, footwork is everything. His moves cannot be static, but should be smooth and flow naturally. A definite rhythm is involved, dictating the necessity of spending ample time every day developing footwork. We like to tell our quarterbacks that they would be in great demand at the high school "hops" because of all the time they spend working on their footwork.

The outside veer is a true triple option, and we simplify the rules for the quarterback in reading the veer. His read is always 3 on the line of scrimmage, and with his opening step, he will locate and lock in on him. If the read stands or comes upfield, he hands the ball off. If the read closes or slants down the line of scrimmage and is not blocked by the tight end, the quarterback will keep the ball, step around the collision, and turn upfield immediately. He must never string the play out toward the sideline, and he will never pitch off 3.

The quarterback is not going to make the proper read 100 percent of the time, but should be able to tell why he did what he did. A general rule of thumb is that when in doubt, hand off. The cardinal rule is that if the read fills the C gap and is not blocked by the tight end ("never hand the ball off"). If he does, the dive back pays the price and a team risks a high possibility of a turnover. Daily drills using defensive ends and linebackers with shields will help him react to the variety of defensive looks faced come game time. These drills are run at game speed, but without full contact.

We have enjoyed our greatest success with the outside veer when we are able to hand the ball off to the dive back. Unlike many veer teams, our quarterback will never pull the ball on any triple option. Once the ball is seated, the dive back will lock on to it even if it means dragging the quarterback downfield with him.

## Reading the Splitside Veer

We do not employ the inside veer in our attack because, in our thinking, it is a difficult read for the quarterback to make successfully and with any degree of consistency. Rather, we run the triple option to the splitside of the formation with a play we simply call the "veer." It is a very quick-hitting play that is a successful part of our overall offensive package. The play puts a lot of pressure on the opponent's defense, so we run it early in the game to see what kind of athlete is lined up there to take it away from us and to determine how they are going to defend the splitside.

To eliminate any stutter or pause step by the quarterback when running the splitside veer, we cheat our running backs up a yard, their heels being four yards from the line of scrimmage. The landmark for the dive back is the outside hip of the playside guard. He will run a 100-yard dash for his landmark with his eyes on the point of attack. The quarterback will open with his playside foot, stepping down the line of scrimmage with his eyes riveted on his read. He reads the defender on, or immediately outside our playside tackle. He will mesh with the dive back on his second step. The quarterback should determine with his first step whether he is going to hand the ball off or keep it. It is a quick read for the quarterback, but not a difficult read for him. If the read stands, plays soft, or comes upfield, he will hand the ball off to the dive back. If the read slants or closes, he will keep the ball and turn upfield immediately.

As with the outside veer, we drill our quarterbacks daily with their footwork and timing in running the splitside veer. This simple play is a major weapon in our offensive arsenal. It is effective anywhere on the field and against most defensive fronts and has been deadly against the "prevent" defense. We especially like to run it when the defense is reduced to our splitside.

In running the triple option, the quarterback must be able to answer any of three basic questions on a given play:
- What did you perceive that prompted you to hand the ball off?
- What did you see that caused you to pitch the football?
- What did you see that caused you to keep the ball?

The quarterback, knowing that his coach will be quizzing him frequently during the practice session, will make a concerted effort to read rather than to simply make a guess, most likely based on his pre-snap read. Although the quarterback is not going to make the correct read all of the time, we want to know why he did what he did in a given situation. It is called accountability and responsibility. The duty of the coach is to make things simple and understandable enough so that the quarterback will experience success with greater frequency than he experiences failure. Confidence in his own ability to read the triple option is paramount to the quarterback's success in executing it. If properly presented and installed, it should be his favorite play in the offense.

## Straight Option Reads

Our regular option package gives us the opportunity to get the ball on the perimeter of the defense with a number of diversified looks. Included are the dive option, con option, crazy option, Pony option, along with the lead and counter-lead options. Each of these options are discussed at length elsewhere in this text, so in this section we will deal mainly with the techniques of the quarterback at the point of attack.

Our quarterback occupies the defender on the line of scrimmage responsible for him on the option. He attacks him at an angle that prevents him from playing off of him and onto the pitchback. On all of the options, quarterbacks are drilled to attack the defender "downhill." He does so by attacking the inside shoulder of the defender, enticing the defender to take him. In a hard look, the quarterback will come under control, pitch the ball immediately, and be prepared to absorb a blow from the defender. If the defender plays soft or feathers, the quarterback steps toward him, getting close enough so that defender must make a play on him. In all cases, the quarterback is under control, attacking his defender at game speed and not throttling down. A cardinal rule for the quarterback is that he should never pitch under duress, but rather keep the football and get what he can.

We coordinate our option drills with all of the drills designed to improve the quarterbacks pitching techniques. Each practice, during individual time, the quarterbacks and running backs work on their execution and timing along with proper pitch phase. We use defensive ends with shields to give the quarterbacks a variety of looks and defensive techniques. Every Tuesday practice is designated as "option night," and we take as much as 25 to 40 minutes running all of our options against defensive ends and linebackers along with a defensive perimeter, affording our quarterbacks the opportunity to face every possible defensive alignment that has been designed to neutralize option football.

It has been our experience that option football is successful in all kinds of weather. Some of our biggest numbers were put up during the worst climatic conditions. With this factor in mind, we take time to practice with wet footballs throughout the season, and inclement weather does not keep us off of the practice field. We practice in the rain and snow because often our games were played on muddy turf and under such conditions. Lightning and earthquakes are, however, two natural phenomena that will definitely keep us indoors and off of the football field.

Figure 3-1. Option football is a great wet-weather offense.

# Offensive Personnel

## Running Backs

A natural progression is followed in the instruction and teaching of the basic stance. Begin with a two-point stance, legs bent comfortably with hands on the knees, feet parallel and approximately shoulder-width apart. Toes point directly ahead while the feet are slightly staggered, one foot ahead of the other. The ideal stagger is a "toe-to-instep" relationship, which may vary per individual, but not exceed a "toe-to-heel" alignment. Subtle adjustments may be necessary, taking into account physical size, body type, and athletic ability.

From the two-point stance, the running back drops into the three-point stance. He does not move his feet, but maintains his foot stagger. If the right foot is back, the right hand comes down with the fingers forming a tripod to balance his stance. The hand is directly below his eyes, weight equally distributed on the balls of the feet, and stabilized on his down hand. The other forearm rests easily on the thigh of his forward leg. Heels are off the ground, his "tail" is high, and knees are directly over the feet. Head alignment is normal and comfortable. He should not crane the neck so as to force the butt down. The running back should just be able to see the heels of the linemen in front of him.

Repetition results in the player's stance becoming natural and routine, and he is able to drop into his stance with ease. Correct stance is a constant and does not vary so as not to tip off the direction of the play. In a proper stance, the player is able to accelerate to the left, the right, straight ahead, or on a veer course with equal success.

## Wide Receivers

Flankers and split ends must accelerate off the ball and drive downfield, so the basic sprinter's stance is employed. Teaching and instruction is thus more efficient because the techniques used are the same as with the running backs. Using the same stance simplifies the interchanging of personnel if numbers are a factor in your program. Although their sprinter's stance is identical to that of the running backs, the wideouts have three "constants" to remember when assuming their stance:
- The outside leg is always back.
- The outside hand is always down.
- Eyes are always looking in toward the center and quarterback because they move on "ball movement."

# Forming the Pocket

Our dive back forms a good pocket to ensure a smooth, clean handoff from the quarterback. He accomplishes this goal by having his inside arm and elbow up just below chin level with his wrist rotated so the thumb points toward the ground while the outside arm rests comfortably across his belt line. His head and eyes are just above the rotated wrist of his upper arm. When the football is seated in the pocket, he closes over the ball, securing it safely in his mid-section. He locks the ball away, protecting it with his body, and does not shift it until he gets into the defensive secondary away from heavy traffic.

# Carrying the Football

Running with the football and protecting it is vital to the success of any offensive scheme. Turnovers, more so than any other factors, can spell disaster for your team. Fumbling can actually become a mindset, so paying careful attention to teaching proper technique is of the utmost importance in preventing a turnover. Players can be taught not to fumble. It must be ingrained daily in their thinking to protect the football at all times. A "cavalier" attitude with the football is unacceptable.

To maximize protection of the football when in the open field, the ball is cradled with the forearm while the hand, thumb, and fingers form a cup over the tip of the ball. Our running backs are coached to "bruise the ribs" by clutching the ball tightly to their torso. We never want to see daylight between the football and the ballcarrier's body.

Constant reminders on protecting the ball, combined with daily ball drills through the "blaster" with teammates clutching and grabbing at the ball, builds confidence and reassurance in the backs' determination to secure the football.

# Shifting the Football

Once in the open field, it is often necessary for the running back to shift the football from one arm to the other, thus protecting it from an onrushing defender. This task is accomplished by reaching the other arm across his body with the hand, thumb, and fingers cupping the opposite end of the football and pulling it smartly across the body, locking it safely away. The football is always in contact with the player's torso, again with our coaches emphasizing the importance of not having any daylight between the ball and the running back's body. We expect our back's jersey to be "soiled" by the mere repetition of shifting the ball from one arm to the other during a normal practice session.

# Audible System

## Description

Although our audible system is simple, it proves to be a successful and integral part of the twin veer offense. Before getting into the rudiments of the system, it is important to note that our audible system is employed primarily to check us out of a play that the defense is aligned to stop. Rather than have our quarterback burdened with the onus of play selection at the line of scrimmage, we want him to be able to, by defensive recognition, determine whether or not the called play has a reasonable probability of success. Once under the center, he checks the defensive alignment, making certain that we are not outnumbered at the point of attack. If he is satisfied that we are not, he will proceed with the play called in the huddle. We do not want our quarterback guessing or trying to outsmart the defense at the line of scrimmage. He has enough to think about ("run the play").

Common sense and simplicity are the cornerstones of the audible system. In the event the quarterback recognized that the defense was overloaded in the area we intended to attack, a simple "opposite" call signals his teammates that we are running the same play, but now to the opposite side of the formation. If the play called in the huddle is Pony option right (toward the twins and the wideside of the field) and the quarterback notes that the defense has overloaded to the twins while the free safety is also cheated over, the success ratio of the play is significantly reduced. Obviously, to run the play is folly and could be courting disaster. At the line of scrimmage, the quarterback yells, "Opposite, opposite," and on the same snap count, the team runs Pony option left.

We coach our quarterbacks to be alert to the possibility that the defense may inadvertently line up incorrectly on a given down, thus exposing a glaring weakness that could be exploited. Often, the successful offensive play is the direct result of a miscue by the defensive unit. Our philosophy of taking advantage of what the defense might give us has resulted in countless big plays over the years.

## Mechanics

Our coaching staff formulates the game plan, and all of our plays are sent in from the sideline via the coaching staff. We feel this method takes undo pressure and stress from the shoulders of a young 17- or 18-year-old who is doing his best to execute the offense.

In the huddle and in our playbook, all of our plays are called by name and not by number. It doesn't take a degree in quantum physics to understand: dive right, pass left, option right, con-dive left, and so on. The phonetic system has functioned very well for us since its inception in 1975. We do, however, employ a simple numbering system to enable us when necessary to check off at the line of scrimmage.

To grasp the workings of our audible system, it is necessary to know the cadence of the quarterback at the line of scrimmage. It is as follows: Team set (pause), then any two-digit number repeated twice, go, one hut, two hut, three hut. For example: Team set, 72, 72, go, one hut, two hut, three hut. The cadence is non-rhythmic, so as not to let the defense anticipate our away count, while affording an opportunity to audible against any last-second maneuvering of the defense. The number in the cadence is meaningless unless it is one of our "hot" numbers. The hot numbers may change from week to week, or they may remain constant.

The next step is to assign a number to each play:
- Running plays: Trap = 0; Slant = 1; Dive = 2; Veer = 3; Option = 5
- Pass plays: Play-action = 7; Half-roll = 8; Roll = 9.

Then, add the hot number to get up and running. For example, this week, the hot numbers are the 20s and the 30s. The 20s designate the plays that will be run to our right, while the 30s designate the plays that will go to our left. Therefore, when the quarterback yells, "22, 22," he is checking to dive right. If he shouts, "33, 33," he is running veer left.

We train our quarterbacks to check off frequently in practice during team scheme so that the entire squad becomes conditioned to and adept at picking the audible calls. All other numerical calls are dummy calls and are meaningless. While the 20s and 30s are "hot," anything in 40s, 50s, 60s, 70s, 80s, or 90s are dummy calls intended for the defense to decipher.

With an audible to a pass play, besides giving the numbers, the quarterback will also call the stunts to be run by the receivers. For example, "29 bench" tells the team that we are running our sprint-out passing look, or "roll right, bench." He could say, "Jet," "In-streak," "Post-snake," "Fly," or any other combination of patterns. More about stunts and patterns for the receivers can be found in Chapter 5.

## Hurry-Up Offense (Condition Red)

Most often, when employing our "hurry-up" attack, we operate against some form of "prevent" defense. Thus, our offense is designed to take advantage of a defense that was both loosened up and spread out. Our aim is to exploit the "soft spots" along the line of scrimmage and in the deepened secondary. Obviously, the goal is to move the football as quickly and efficiently as possible into scoring position, be it a touchdown or a field goal—always looking for points. Our approach involves utilizing the quick outs and hitches, combined with crossing patterns intermixed with a varied ground attack. The success of any two-minute offense is generally dependent upon satisfying a number of criteria. These criteria will vary with individual programs, but the following is a set of guidelines we use in installing our attack:

- It should be simple enough for all to understand, thus allowing for ease of implementation and execution.
- It should have some degree of complexity and be vast enough to be able to attack all areas of the opponent's defense.
- It should coincide completely with the overall philosophy of the total offensive scheme.
- As with any other learned response, it must be practiced frequently under controlled game conditions that include down-and-distance, time remaining, time-outs available, field position, and field conditions.

## Rules

The rules governing the two-minute offense are brief and simple. Given that this offense is a no-huddle offense, all players must be alert to the transitions and sudden changes that are always occurring around them. They must be particularly alert as to the status of the game clock. Is the clock stopped, or does it continue to run? Vital seconds can be lost or saved by heads-up play. Following are the guidelines for our two-minute attack with the clock running:

- Players always line up in the twins formation.
- Twins will always align to the wideside of the field.
- The backs and linemen will immediately line up on the ball in their down position.
- The football is always snapped on "Go." The cadence is, "Ready, go."
- Running backs and receivers get as much yardage as they can, and then get out of bounds to stop the clock.
- The audible at the line of scrimmage is: the play call, then "Ready, go."

A sample play call at the line might be: "25 lead, 25 lead, ready, go." This call will indicate to the team that we are running lead option right on go. When the clock is stopped, the players huddle as usual with the play sent in from the sideline.

Whatever system you decide to use in the two-minute game, be certain to keep it simple. Sell the players on what you are trying to accomplish with it, and be sure to practice it repeatedly throughout the season. During the practice session on the day preceding a game, it is a given that the hurry-up offense will take up a significant portion of your preparation time.

# Motion

Motion affords us the opportunity to camouflage the set we are running from by lining up in one formation then motioning into another. We employ three basic motions involving the flanker back in our attack: flat motion, deep motion, and short motion. Terminology used in designating them are: *flipper* for flat motion, which is long motion across the formation; *flip* for deep motion into our backfield; and *short flip* for short motion, used in isolations and quick passes. A fourth motion involves the running backs and is called *bravo right* or *left*. It is a simple, convenient method to get into a trips formation with little or no transitional problems.

When motion is called in this system, we line up in a set opposite of the set intended to be run. The quarterback calls the set in the huddle and motions to it. For example, the quarterback calls "Bayport right, flipper, option right," and the team will line up in a pro left set. After setting the team, the quarterback signals motion to the flanker, who then motions across the formation to the twins-right look.

The opposite is true if we intend to run from a pro set using motion. We line up in our twins formation and motion to the pro set. In either case, the width of the flanker's motion is controlled by the cadence of the quarterback.

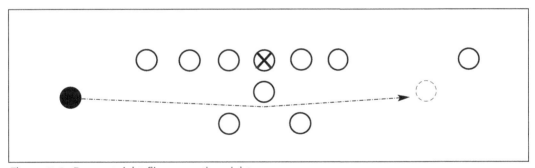

Figure 3-2. Bayport right flipper, option right

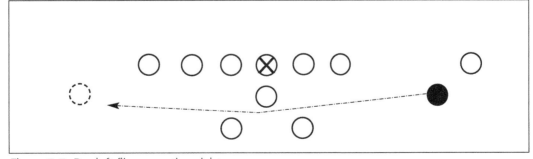

Figure 3-3. Pro left flipper, option right

The same rules utilized in flipper motion also apply to flip motion. The squad lines up opposite the call made in the huddle and motions toward our intended set. Flip or deep motion allows us to get our flanker into position to become a third running back or be a lead back on the isolation. It also gives a three-back lead on the quarterback power sweep, which in our terminology is called "roll, live."

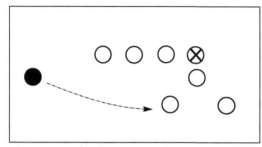

Figure 3-4. Flip (pro to twins)

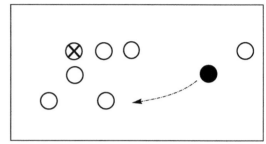

Figure 3-5. Flip (twins to pro)

The short-flip motion differs from the previously described motions in that we line up in the formation called in the huddle. It affords an opportunity to motion from a normal twins formation to a slot look and to a pro set with a tight flanker. It is used to gain an advantage in setting up blocking angles and is effective in changing the look of our passing game.

Bravo motion puts one of two running backs in motion and leaves a one-back set. It quickly allows a team to motion into trips from both the twins set and the pro set and affords the opportunity to roll to the trips with a lead back or to counter and trap back to the weakside. When running bravo motion, the running back opposite the call is the motion back. If the quarterback calls, "Bayport right, bravo right," the left running back will set and then go in motion to his right.

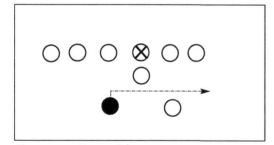

Figure 3-6. Bravo right

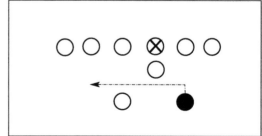

Figure 3-7. Bravo left

# 4

# The Running Attack

The base play of the Bayport veer offense is the hard dive or the called dive. It is the very first play we put into our scheme on day one. Through the years, it has been our most consistent ground gainer. This play helps develop the "smashmouth" type of thinking in players that is so important in our run-oriented attack. The basic concept of the dive is to create the illusion of width for the defense and the appearance of attacking outside while we are, in fact, running inside.

## Hard Dive

The hard dive is a four-step move for the quarterback that calls for him to mesh with the dive back on his third step. The dive back's landmark is the inside hip of the onside tackle. The play is simple in context, but complex in execution. We tell our players that we just don't run a dive play, but that the called dive is a read situation for the dive back. The handoff is deep enough and allows the back to read the blocks ahead of him and run to daylight.

A worst-case scenario when running the called dive is to commit the ballcarrier to a designated gap. If the hole is not there, he will be stopped for no gain or a loss of yardage. A critical coaching point arises with the quarterback's third step at the mesh point with the dive back. The quarterback must not force the dive back into the B gap. Instead, his fourth step will involve using a "limp leg." We tell him to be like a toreador, allowing the dive back to "run with his eyes," thus enabling him to run "where they aren't."

## Quarterback Assignments and Rules

- The first step is an open step with his playside foot. His second step is a crossover step with his opposite foot, which will align him just behind the offensive guard. The third step is a 45-degree angle back toward the dive back. He extends his arms, reaching back to ensure a deep handoff.
- The quarterback's fourth step is critical. His eyes are fixed on the point of attack, allowing him to guide the dive back into the opening.
- After meshing with the dive back, the quarterback rides him hip-deep, then detaches.
- The quarterback continues down the line of scrimmage, carrying out his option fakes.

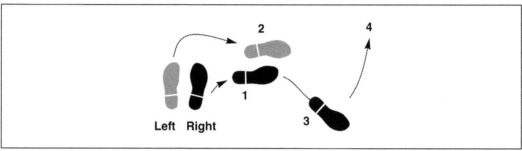

Figure 4-1. The hard dive—quarterback footwork

## Dive Back Assignments and Rules

- The first two steps of the dive back are at less than full speed.
- He open steps with his playside foot and then executes a crossover step with his opposite foot.
- The third step will turn him up the hole and square his shoulders parallel to the line of scrimmage.
- As he meshes with the quarterback and receives the football, the dive back accelerates at game speed toward his landmark.
- Reading the blocks in front of him, he follows the course of least resistance and looks for the seam that will break him loose. He may end up running the B gap, or it may look like the cutback dive.

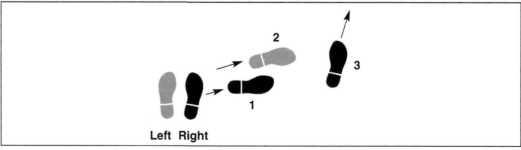

Figure 4-2. Dive back footwork

## Pitchback Assignments and Rules

- The pitchback simulates the action used in the dive option.
- He open steps with his playside foot.
- His second step is a crossover step that will put him in pitch phase with the quarterback.
- The pitchback continues down the line of scrimmage, making the defense read option.

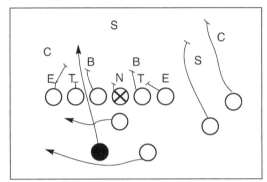

Figure 4-3. Dive 52 Eagle

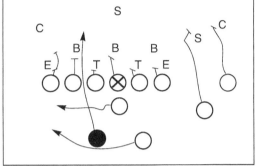

Figure 4-4. Dive 4-3

# Outside Veer

The companion play to the hard dive is the outside veer. It is the second play installed in our attack. We feel that this play puts tremendous pressure on the defense because it is the true triple option. Through the years, we have found that opposing teams have "stacked" their defenses to take away our outside veer. This reason alone makes it a valuable tool in our offense because if they outman us there, we are able to attack them elsewhere. Our outside veer can only be run to the tight-end side of our formation because we need the block of the tight end to the inside. We have our greatest success with this play when we are able to hand off to our dive back. When our quarterback is able to keep the ball and turn up on the corner back, we bring out the extra-point team.

## Quarterback Assignments and Rules

- Our quarterback will open step with the playside foot, keeping the football at the "ready position" and the tip of the ball pointed directly at his read.
- He accelerates down the line of scrimmage, fixing his eyes on the defender he is reading (the read is 3 on the line of scrimmage). He will mesh with the dive back between his third and fourth steps and will determine whether to keep or to hand off by his second step.

- If the read stands or plays soft, he will hand the ball off.
- If the read closes or slants down the line of scrimmage, he will step around the collision and turn immediately upfield. Never string the play out to the sideline.
- The quarterback must work directly along the line of scrimmage—if he bows back, the play will fail.
- He never seats the ball in the running back's pocket unless he intends to hand it off. (We never pull the ball when running the veer.)
- We never pitch off 3.

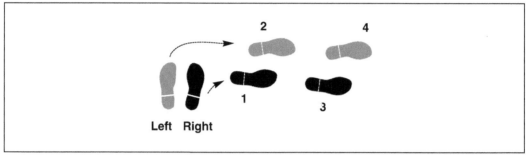

Figure 4-5. Outside veer—quarterback footwork

## Dive Back Assignments and Rules

- The first step for the dive back is an open step directly at his landmark, which is the outside hip of the offensive tackle.
- Then, it is a 100-yard dash toward the point of attack with eyes focused upon the landmark. (Never look for the ball.)
- If he feels the ball at the mesh point, the dive back "locks" onto it even if it means dragging the quarterback with him.
- He must expect to break arm tackles at the line of scrimmage and BYOB (be your own blocker).
- The dive back never deviates from his course until he has the football. He will "run with his eyes."

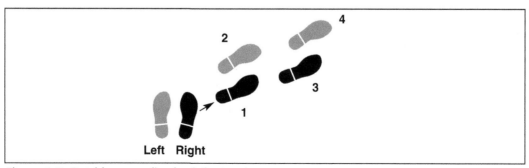

Figure 4-6. Outside veer—dive back footwork

## Pitchback Assignments and Rules

- The pitchback's first step is a crossover step playside, and it is very important to get away at game speed.
- He maintains pitch phase with the quarterback while keeping a five-yard cushion.
- He is prepared to turn upfield simultaneously with the quarterback and be alert for the sudden pitch.
- He continues to maintain pitch phase downfield as the quarterback may be able to pitch off the corner.

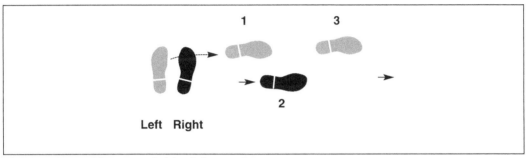

Figure 4-7. Outside veer—pitchback footwork

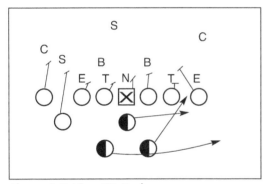

Figure 4-8. Veer 52 Eagle

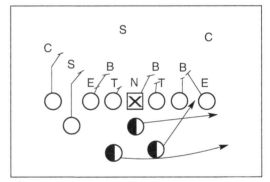

Figure 4-9. Veer 4-3

# Slant

The slant is the third running play of our inside package. In reality, the cutback dive is intended to take advantage of the fast flow of the opposing linebackers. The strategy of the play involves a deep handoff to the running back, thus allowing him to read the key blocks of the center and playside guard. As with the hard dive, the quarterback must step accordingly so as not to force the ballcarrier into a designated gap.

The landmark for the dive back is dictated by the alignment of the defensive front. In an odd front, with the center covered, the landmark is directly over the butt of the center. With an even front, and both of our guards covered, the destination will be straight ahead over the playside guard. In the event that all three (the center and both guards) are covered, the landmark is the butt of the playside guard. Although we have run the slant successfully against this defensive look after identifying this alignment at the line of scrimmage, we prefer to check to a different call. We have great success with this play against hard rushing, pursuit-type defenses. The slant sets up two companion plays: the quarterback follow and the crazy option.

## Quarterback Assignments and Rules

- The quarterback's first step is a drop step with his backside foot to attain depth and to clear the path for the dive back, whose landmark is the butt of the center (assuming we are attacking an "odd front").
- His second step is a long stride with his playside foot directly toward the dive back.
- With his second step, the quarterback extends his arms, meshing with the dive back, thus ensuring a deep handoff.
- The third step is a ride step, guiding the running to his landmark. He will ride the dive back hip-deep toward the line of scrimmage before detaching.
- After the handoff, the quarterback will continue his footwork to his left, faking the crazy option along the line of scrimmage.

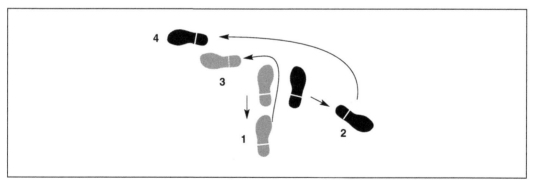

Figure 4-10. Slant—quarterback footwork

## Dive Back Assignments and Rules

- The dive back's initial step is directly at his landmark, which is the butt of the center in an odd front or the butt of the guard in an overlook.
- On his second step, with eyes fixed on his landmark, he meshes with the quarterback while reading the block of the center if an odd front, or the block of the on guard if an even front.
- The dive back must "run with his eyes" and be prepared to make a quick cut against fast-flowing linebackers.

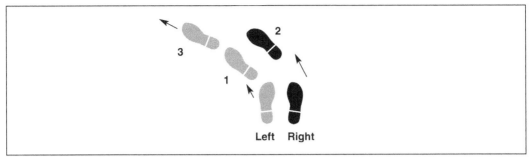

Figure 4-11. Slant—dive back footwork

## Pitchback Assignments and Rules

- The pitchback's first step is an open step playside with his right foot.
- The second step is a crossover step with his left foot, making it appear that he is getting into pitch for option right.
- On the crossover, he plants the left foot, shifting the weight to that foot while executing a whirley move, which involves turning the head and shoulders away from the line of scrimmage and then continuing to our offensive left, faking the crazy option.
- The pitchback has his head "on a swivel" while executing the whirley, then stays in pitch phase with the quarterback, who is also faking the crazy option.

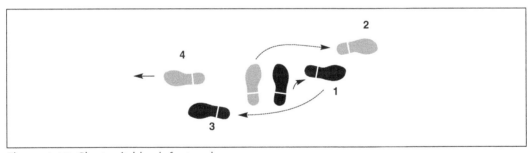

Figure 4-12. Slant—pitchback footwork

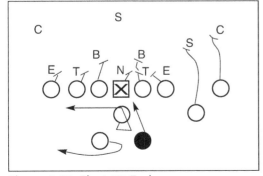

Figure 4-13. Slant 52 Eagle

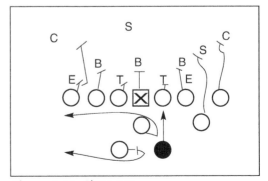

Figure 4-14. Slant 4-3

# Quarterback Follow

The quarterback follow mirrors the cutback dive in all aspects, except the quarterback is the ballcarrier rather than the dive back. The landmark for the dive back remains constant, as does the blocking scheme for the linemen. Footwork for all involved is identical to the footwork for the slant. This is a low risk play because it does not involve a handoff of any kind, and we gain an additional blocker, the dive back. It is similar to a quarterback isolation, but with a slight delay by the ballcarrier.

## Quarterback Assignments and Rules

- The quarterback's initial footwork is identical to the footwork previously described for the slant. His first step is a drop step with his backside foot to attain depth and to clear the path for the dive back, whose landmark is the butt of the center (assuming we are attacking an "odd front").
- His second step is a long stride with his playside foot directly toward the dive back.
- With his second step, the quarterback extends his arms, meshing with the dive back, thus ensuring a deep handoff.
- The third step is a ride step, guiding the running to his landmark. He will ride the dive back hip-deep toward the line of scrimmage before detaching.
- Upon meshing with the dive back, he rides the dive back and pulls the ball after riding him hip-deep.
- The quarterback takes a brief pause to let the dive back clear, and then follows him up the hole, running to daylight.

## Dive Back Assignments and Rules

- The dive back's initial step is directly at his landmark, which is the butt of the center in an odd front or the butt of the guard in an overlook.
- On his second step, with eyes fixed on his landmark, he meshes with the quarterback while reading the block of the center if an odd front, or the block of the on guard if an even front.
- Upon detaching from the quarterback, he sinks a great fake with his eyes fixed on the point of attack.
- If not tackled, he blocks the most dangerous defender in his path. If no one is there, he goes to the next level.

## Pitchback Assignments and Rules

- The pitchback's first step is an open step playside with his right foot.

- The second step is a crossover step with his left foot, making it appear that he is getting into pitch for option right.
- On the crossover, he plants the left foot, shifting the weight to that foot while executing a whirley move, which involves turning the head and shoulders away from the line of scrimmage and then continuing to our offensive left, faking the crazy option.
- The pitchback has his head "on a swivel" while executing the whirley, then stays in pitch phase with the quarterback, who is also faking the crazy option.
- He then fakes the option.

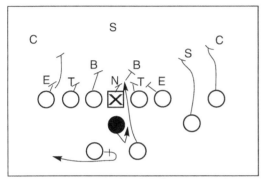

Figure 4-15. Quarterback follow 52 Eagle

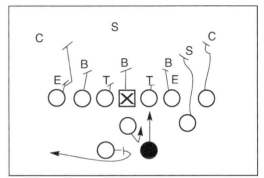

Figure 4-16. Quarterback follow 4-3

# Trap

The trap is a fast-hitting inside play that allows us to attack the middle, using a slightly different look. In our system, when running the trap play, we name the play by telling our guards which direction we are trapping. Trap right tells the left guard to execute a trap technique to his right. He will trap the first down defensive lineman, removed from center. The trap is the only inside hitting play in our play book where the running back, opposite the play call, ends up being the ballcarrier. The trap enables us to keep the defense honest and still allows us to take advantage of an aggressive and active defense. The trap play sets up our Pony option play.

**Quarterback Assignments and Rules**

- The first step is a drop step with his playside foot. The drop step gives the quarterback depth and clears the running lane for the dive back
- The second step is a long stride with his opposite foot, meshing with the left dive back as deeply as possible.
- During the second step, the quarterback extends his arms, ensuring a deep handoff, allowing the dive back to follow the trapping guard.

- With arms extended, the quarterback seats the football and rides the dive back hip-deep toward the line of scrimmage.
- After the handoff, the quarterback continues to attack down the line of scrimmage, faking the Pony option.

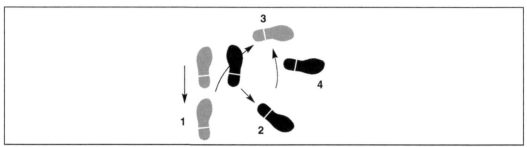

Figure 4-17. Trap—quarterback footwork

## Dive Back Assignments and Rules

- The dive back's first step is with the inside foot directly at his landmark, which is always the butt of the center.
- He meshes with the quarterback on the second step, three yards behind the line of scrimmage.
- He reads the block of the trapping guard, knowing that he will trap the first down lineman removed from center.
- He is aware that the hole will be wider versus an odd front and closer to the center versus the even front.

## Pitchback Assignments and Rules

- The first step is an open step with the playside foot, slightly back for depth.
- The second step is a crossover step, getting the pitchback into pitch phase.
- The first three steps are at less than full speed to allow the quarterback and dive back to mesh and ride until the handoff is made.
- He stays in proper pitch phase with the quarterback, who is also faking the Pony option.

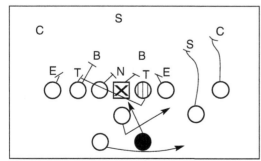

Figure 4-18. Trap 52 Eagle

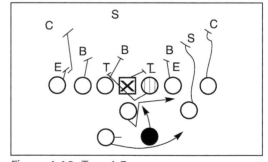

Figure 4-19. Trap 4-3

# Splitside Veer

The veer to the splitside of our formation is the quickest hitting play in our playbook. It puts great pressure on the outside defender on the line of scrimmage. We would go to this play early during our first series with the football to determine how the defense is geared to stop it. We also find out what type of athlete is lined up there to take this play away from our attack.

The split veer is the only play in our attack where we cheat our running backs up closer to the line of scrimmage. For this play, the backs line up with their heels four yards behind the tip of the football, rather than five. This play is effective most anytime during the course of the game, but quite often deadly on long-yardage situations and against a prevent look when the defense is aligned to take away the pass. A quick back in the opponent's secondary can create great scoring opportunities. We had our best success with the split veer when we were able to make the handoff. The split veer is the true triple option and puts tremendous pressure on the defense.

## Quarterback Assignments and Rules

- The quarterback reads the defender lined up on, or immediately outside of, the offensive tackle.
- He open steps with his playside foot, stepping directly toward his read, while keeping his eyes fixed on him.
- The quarterback must make his read during his first two steps.
- His second step is a crossover step, which will put him just behind the playside guard.
- His mesh point is at the outside hip of the on guard. We are running at the B gap, but shading the inside of the gap.
- Steps three and four are adjustment steps, dictated by the reaction of the defender.
- The quarterback's rule for reading the split veer is: if the read stands or charges upfield, hand the ball off.
- If the read closes or slants down, his rule is: keep the ball, step around the collision, and be prepared to turn upfield. He should never seat the ball to the dive back and then pull it.

## Dive Back Assignments and Rules

- His heels are aligned at four yards behind the tip of the football.
- His landmark is the B gap, but hugging the outside hip of the guard.
- His first step is an open step with the playside foot directly at his landmark.

- He runs a 100-yard dash at the landmark with his eyes fixed on the point of attack.
- The dive back will clamp onto the football if he feels it placed in his pocket, even if he drags the quarterback with him.
- The dive back must be prepared to break an arm tackle at the line of scrimmage.

## Pitchback Assignments and Rules

- The first step is a crossover step with the foot opposite playside.
- The second step with the playside foot is a lateral step to get depth to get into pitch phase.
- He maintains pitch phase with the quarterback by keeping a five-yard cushion; he should be ready to turn upfield with the quarterback and be prepared for the sudden pitch.

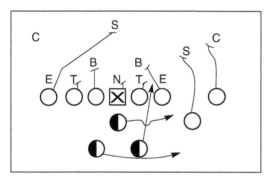

Figure 4-20. Split veer 52 Eagle

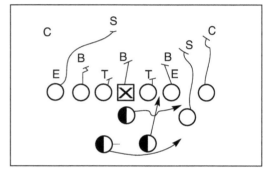

Figure 4-21. Split veer 4-3

# Isolation

The isolation is one the few true power plays in our offensive package. It enables us to get a double-team at the point of attack, while using a running back as an additional blocker. This play involves a deep handoff to the running back, enabling him to adjust to the blocks ahead of him. Our backfield movement begins with the same action as the rest of our offense in order not to tip off the defense as to the direction we intend to attack. The isolation sets up our bootleg and misdirection look.

## Quarterback Assignments and Rules

- The quarterback's first step is an open step with the playside foot.
- His second step is a crossover step with the opposite foot, which will align him directly behind the on guard.
- The third step is with the playside foot straight back toward the running back.

- Between his third and fourth steps, the quarterback will mesh with the dive back and execute his handoff. The quarterback is facing away from the line of scrimmage while making the handoff.
- The fifth and ensuing quarterback steps are away from playside, getting depth, and setting him on a bootleg course. He sprints along this route, "hipping" the football, while looking downfield for a potential receiver.

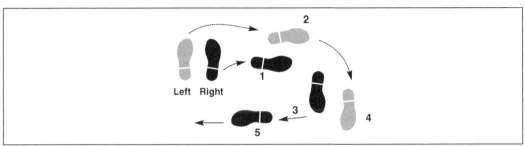

Figure 4-22. Quarterback footwork

## Isolation Back Assignments and Rules

- On a pre-snap read, he visually locates the linebacker he is responsible for.
- With the snap, he sprints directly at the linebacker to be blocked. No fake is necessary.
- He occupies the linebacker with an explosion-type block: "to him and through him."

## Pitchback Assignments and Rules

- The pitchback's first step is an open step with the playside foot.
- The second step is a crossover step, seemingly putting him into pitch phase.
- The third step is with the playside foot; he plants, and then turns sharply upfield.
- He meshes with the quarterback between the third and fourth steps, reading the double-team at the point of attack.
- He runs with his eyes and is prepared to cut off the block of the isolation back.

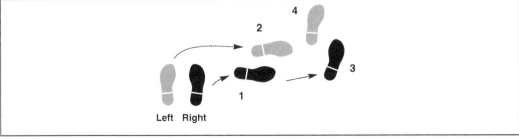

Figure 4-23. Pitchback footwork

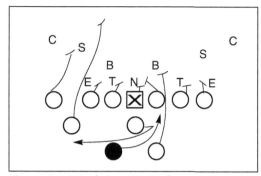

Figure 4-24. Isolation 52 Eagle

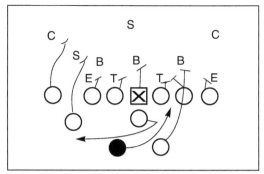

Figure 4-25. Isolation 4-3

# Counter Dive

Due to the success of the hard dive, the counter dive has been very productive and is a mainstay in the total offensive scheme. It complements the rest of the inside running game and sets up its companion play, the counter option. The counter dive gives a quick hitter, combined with a misdirection look. It has been particularly effective against quick reacting and fast-flowing linebackers. The misdirection "freezes" the linebackers, giving our linemen better blocking angles. The counter dive is designed to attack the guard-center gap, but the handoff is made deep enough to allow the dive back to read and run to daylight.

## Quarterback Assignments and Rules

- For counter dive right, the footwork of the quarterback is called "replacement footwork."
- The first step is an open step away from playside with the left foot.
- The second step will bring the right foot parallel with the left foot, thus balancing him up. The quarterback has the ball in the ready position, but is showing it to the defense.
- His third step is with the left foot, back toward the playside, aligning him just behind the center.
- The handoff is made, with arms extended, to the dive back between the third and fourth steps.
- Care must be taken by the quarterback not to force the dive back wider than his intended landmark (A gap).
- After the handoff, he finishes by continuing down the line of scrimmage, faking the counter option.

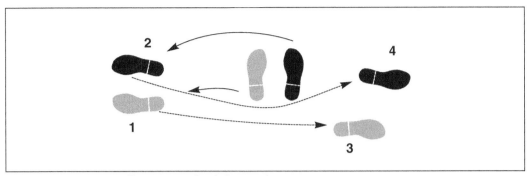

Figure 4-26. Counter dive—quarterback footwork

## Dive Back Assignments and Rules

- The first step is an open step with the left foot away from playside, making it appear that the dive back is going into pitch phase. His first step will align him with the A gap.
- The second step is with the right foot to balance up.
- The third step, again with the right foot, is back toward playside and slightly forward.
- He meshes with the quarterback between the third and fourth steps with his eyes riveted on the landmark.
- He accelerates fully on the fourth and ensuing steps, hitting straight ahead.

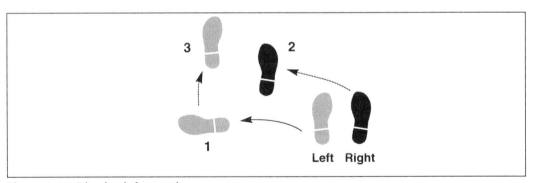

Figure 4-27. Dive back footwork

## Pitchback Assignments and Rules

- The first step is with the left foot, straight ahead, "selling" the hard dive.
- After shifting body weight to the left foot, the second step with the right foot is lateral and slightly back to gain depth. This step is toward playside.
- The third and ensuing steps are made to get into pitch phase with the quarterback, who is also faking the counter option.

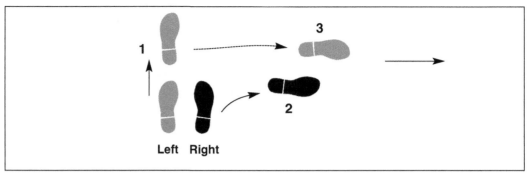

Figure 4-28. Pitchback footwork

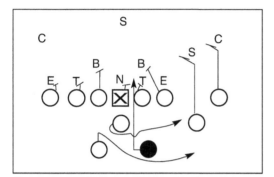

Figure 4-29. Counter dive 52 Eagle

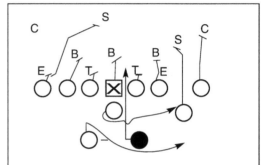

Figure 4-30. Counter dive 4-3

# Load

The load scheme is a low-risk, power-type play, which does not involve a handoff or a pitch. It affords a team an opportunity to execute a running play with the ball in the hands of one of team's best athletes. By design, it is a keeper play for the quarterback and is always run to the tight-end side of the formation. It is the equivalent of an outside isolation play. With the exception of the tight end, the blocking rules are identical to those of the outside veer. In the normal load blocking scheme, the tight end will set up the defensive end for the playside dive back to finish off, then will block to the inside. Two variations of the blocking scheme up front are designated as load-in and load-out. The "in" and "out" calls tell the dive back whether to block inside or outside and may be called at the line of scrimmage.

## Quarterback Assignments and Rules

- He open steps with the playside foot in the direction the play is being run.
- He moves down the line of scrimmage at less than full speed, with the ball at the ready position and eyes on the point of attack.
- Making no fake, he allows dive back to clear, then reads his block and cuts accordingly.

## Dive Back Assignments and Rules

- First step is with the playside foot in the direction of the landmark, the outside hip of the tackle.
- With eyes fixed on the defender to be blocked, he sprints directly at the defender.
- He blocks (in or out, if designated) aggressively to him and through him.

## Pitchback Assignments and Rules

- Footwork and execution are identical to that of the outside veer. He maintains pitch phase with the quarterback and turns upfield when the quarterback does.

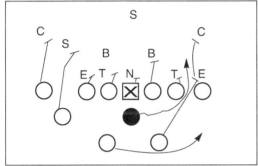

Figure 4-31. Load 52 Eagle

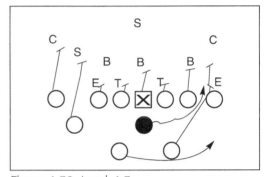

Figure 4-32. Load 4-3

# Dive Option

The dive option is the companion play to the called or hard dive. Because of the great success enjoyed with the hard dive and the sheer number of times we ran it, the dive option has been our most consistent play in successfully getting the football onto the perimeter. We simply call the play option right or option left. The footwork for the quarterback, dive back, and pitchback is identical to the footwork in the hard dive with the same mesh points and landmarks.

With eyes glued on the defender, the quarterback is going to option. He will seat the ball into the pocket formed by the dive back, ride him hip-deep, and then detach. He must be alert for the quick, slanting move of the read, detach immediately, and be prepared to make the sudden pitch. The dive back, after detaching from the quarterback, folds over, making the great fake, and then dips his inside shoulder to hide the fact that he does not have the ball. If given a soft look, the quarterback continues down the line of scrimmage, attacking the defender's inside shoulder. The quarterbacks are trained to never pitch the football while under duress.

## Quarterback Assignments and Rules

- He executes the same three-step move as in the hard dive, but on his first step, the quarterback will fix his eyes on the defender to be optioned.
- He meshes with the dive back on the third step, seats the ball on his inside hip, and rides him hip-deep; then, he detaches and attacks the inside shoulder of the read.
- He is prepared to separate and detach from the dive back quickly if the read pinches or closes hard.
- After the quarterback makes his fake, adjustment steps will put him in position to make the option. He does not throttle down.
- He is prepared to cut up and keep the ball or make the pitch.
- He does not string the option out to the sideline. He challenges the read.

## Dive Back Assignments and Rules

- He executes the same three-step move as is the hard dive.
- He meshes with the quarterback on the third step, folds over the ball, making a great fake.
- The dive back "hugs" the fake and dips his inside shoulder after the quarterback detaches.
- He looks like a ballcarrier, and if not tackled, he becomes a blocker.

## Pitchback Assignments and Rules

- He executes the same footwork as in the hard dive.
- It is the pitchback's responsibility to stay in sync with the quarterback. If he throttles down, the pitchback will throttle down, and so on.
- He sprints toward the sideline, maintaining a five-yard cushion with the quarterback.
- He is prepared for the sudden pitch or the poorly pitched ball. He is ready to turn upfield when the quarterback turns up.

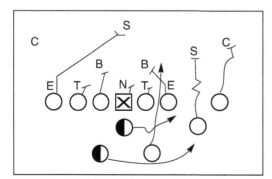

Figure 4-33. Dive option 52 Eagle

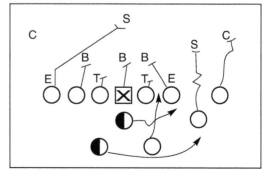

Figure 4-34. Dive option 4-3

# Pony Option

The Pony option is the companion play to the trap. In contrast to the dive option, the Pony option provides a deeper inside fake to our dive back, thus freezing the rapidly pursuing linebackers. Through the years, the Pony option has often been our "go-to" play to successfully get the ball on the perimeter. The deep fake, combined with a longer "ride" to our dive back, resembles the old belly series of the 1960s. One of the advantages of the Pony option is that it gives the quarterback more time to read the defender he is to option. The quarterback will drop step, then step deep toward the dive back that is sprinting at his landmark, the butt of the center. While the quarterback is riding the dive back to his landmark, his eyes are riveted on the defensive end. The quarterback will execute his attack on that defender, the same as in all of our options.

## Quarterback Assignments and Rules

- He executes the same footwork as in the trap. He drop steps with the foot away from playside, while keeping your eyes on the defender to be optioned.
- He takes a long stride with the playside foot (at a 45-degree angle) back toward the dive back.
- He meshes with the dive back on second step, rides him back toward the line of scrimmage, and detaches at hip depth.
- As in all options, the same rules apply when attacking the defender. He always attacks the defender's inside shoulder and attacks downhill; he should be prepared to cut upfield or to make the sudden pitch. (Refer to the description of the footwork for the trap earlier in this chapter.)

## Dive Back Assignments and Rules

- He executes the same footwork as in the trap.
- His landmark is always the butt of the center.
- His first step is directly at the landmark, while meshing with the quarterback on the second step.
- With the second and ensuing steps, he runs a 100-yard dash at the landmark.
- He makes a great fake, then dips the inside shoulder.

## Pitchback Assignments and Rules

- He executes the same footwork as in the trap. The first two steps are at less than full speed.
- He reads the action of the quarterback and react accordingly. He maintains a five-yard cushion while staying in pitch phase. He should not get too far ahead of the quarterback.

Figure 4-35. Running to daylight

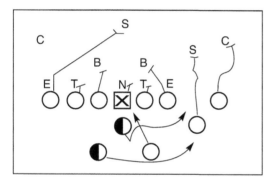
Figure 4-36. Pony option 52 Eagle

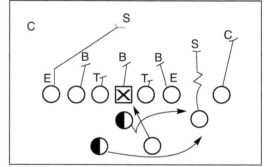
Figure 4-37. Pony option 4-3

## Crazy Option

The crazy option is the companion play of the slant or cutback dive. It adds dimension to the veer attack in that it gives an additional way to attack the perimeter. We call this play "crazy" for lack of a better name. In reality, the backfield movement is a whirley move for our pitchback and an inward move toward the line of scrimmage for our quarterback. The play also gives us a deep inside fake, combined with a misdirection look. This play has been effective to both sides of our formation and has been particularly effective to the splitside of our set. In our flex set, we are able to exploit both sides of the formation with equal success. Our quarterbacks prefer the crazy option to the splitside because we generally get a hard look from the defensive end, dictating the pitch. It is an easy read and is usually a successful play.

When attacking the tight-end side of the formation, the quarterback must accelerate down the line of scrimmage so he does not to get caught from backside pursuit. When we run the slant play, the quarterbacks read what is happening to the defense as they carry out their fakes. If they perceive that the crazy option is open, they signal to the sidelines, and we follow up with the play.

## Quarterback Assignments and Rules

- He executes the same footwork as with the slant. The first step is a drop step with the playside foot (Figure 4-10).
- The second step is a long stride with the foot opposite playside toward the dive back
- On the second step, with arms extended, he meshes with the dive back.
- The third step is a "ride" step, taking the dive back to his landmark, the butt of the center.
- As the quarterback rides his fake, he must snap his head and eyes back to playside to quickly pick up his read. (Note: On all counter moves, the quarterback must have his head on a "swivel" when coming back to playside.)
- He should be ready to detach and pitch quickly because the defensive end is usually in your face.
- If we get a soft look, he attacks as per rule.

## Dive Back Assignments and Rules

- He executes the same footwork as with the slant.
- The landmark is always the butt of the center on the crazy option.
- He runs a 100-yard dash at the landmark.
- He makes a great fake and then becomes a blocker.

## Pitchback Assignments and Rules

- He executes the same footwork as with the slant.
- After the second step, he turns his head and shoulders away from the line of scrimmage (i.e., executes a whirley move).
- In whirley movement, his head is on a "swivel," and he is looking for a hard slanting defender. He should be prepared for a quick pitch from the quarterback.

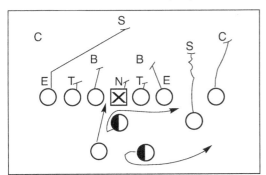

Figure 4-38. Crazy option 52 Eagle

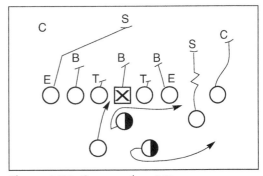

Figure 4-39. Crazy option 4-3

# Counter Option

In a grinding ground attack when you are hammering out four yards and a pint of blood, the misdirection play becomes a necessity. Our counter dive has been such an important part of our offense, and it has paved the way for its companion play, the counter option. With the counter option, we get the inside fake combined with a misdirection look, affording us one more way to attack the outside.

Again, while this play has been successful to both sides of our set, it has been particularly successful to the tight-end side of our formation. Attacking the tight-end side gives our quarterback more room to read as he moves along the line of scrimmage. He must take care, however, to avoid getting run down from the backside.

When attacking the splitside of the formation with this option, the quarterback must be ready to handle a hard slanting defensive end. As he turns back to the playside on his third step, the quarterback should be prepared to make a quick pitch to his pitchback.

## Quarterback Assignments and Rules

- He executes the same footwork as with the counter dive. The first two steps are away from playside (Figure 4-26).
- Upon completion of the second step, he snaps the head and shoulders back to playside, while making the third step, and locates the read.
- He shows the football, but keeps it at the ready position, allowing the dive back to sink the great fake.
- He should be prepared for a hard slanting defensive end and be ready to make the quick pitch.
- If given a soft look, he attacks the inside shoulder of the defender. He should always attack downhill and never bow back or string the play out to the sideline.

## Dive Back Assignments and Rules

- He executes the same footwork as with the counter dive.
- The first step is an open step away from playside, followed by a balance step.
- The third step is directly at the landmark, which is the playside A gap.
- He runs a 100-yard dash at the landmark, making a great fake.
- If not tackled, he becomes a blocker.

## Pitchback Assignments and Rules

- He executes the same footwork as with the counter dive.

- Steps one and two are away from playside. On step three, he rotates his head and shoulders away from the line of scrimmage.
- His head should be on a swivel, ready for the quick pitch.
- He maintains pitch phase with the quarterback as play settles out.

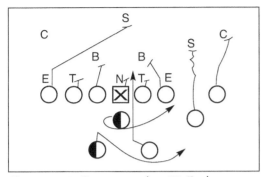

Figure 4-40. Counter option 52 Eagle

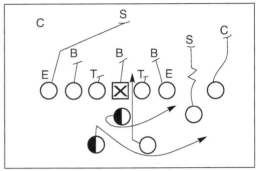

Figure 4-41. Counter option 4-3

# Lead Option

For our quarterback, the lead option is the easiest option for him to execute because it does not entail a fake of any kind. With the snap of the football, the quarterback locates the defender to be optioned and attacks him downhill. The advantage of the lead option over other options in our offensive package is that we get an additional blocker at the point of attack. When the defender responsible for pitch support is shaded inside, our flanker is unable to block him. The lead option solves this situation by having our playside running back become the lead blocker and take on the man coming up to take away our pitchback. It is best to run this play to the wideside of the field and to a two-receiver set. It complements its companion play, the halfback option pass.

### Quarterback Assignments and Rules

- He drop steps with the foot opposite playside and locates the man to be optioned.
- The second step is a balance step to bring the playside foot parallel to the other foot.
- He attacks (downhill) the inside shoulder of the defender to be optioned. He sprints directly at him and does not throttle down.
- He should be prepared to cut upfield or to pitch the football. He should not string out.

### Lead Back Assignments and Rules

- He open steps with his playside foot in the direction play is being run. He locates the defender responsible for pitch support and keeps him in his sights.

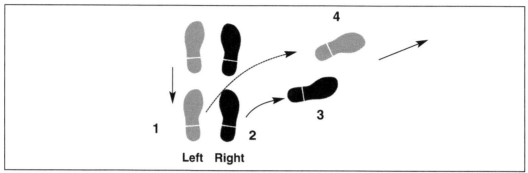

Figure 4-42. Lead option—quarterback footwork

- He sprints an arc path, taking the shortest route to the man assigned to our pitchback.
- He does not throttle down when making his block. It is an aggressive "to him and through him" block.
- As he approaches the defender, he gets in close, "steps on his feet," and explodes into him.
- He should be under control enough so that he does not to allow the defender to side step his block. He should never lunge at the defender.

## Pitchback Assignments and Rules

- He open steps with the playside foot in the direction the play is going.
- He sprints an arc path, following the lead blocker. He should follow the blocker as though he is making footprints in the snow. The blocker will take the pitchback to the end zone.
- He maintains a five-yard cushion while staying in pitch phase with the quarterback.
- He should be prepared for the quick pitch or the poorly executed pitch.

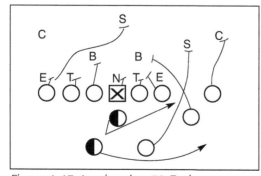

Figure 4-43. Lead option 52 Eagle

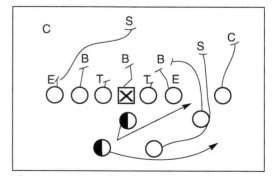

Figure 4-44. Lead option 4-3

# Counter Lead Option

The counter lead option is the lead option with a misdirection look. It has the advantage of freezing the linebackers, thus giving our blockers better blocking angles on them. Although we favored running the lead option to the wideside and two-receiver side of our formation, we have had great success running the counter lead option to the short side of the field toward our tight end. When running either of our lead plays, our flanker or our tight end (depending on the direction of the play) is responsible for sealing to the inside. If the inside is already sealed off, they go on to the next level.

## Quarterback Assignments and Rules

- Steps are identical to steps in the counter dive and counter option, with the exception that no fake is necessary (Figure 4-26).
- With any counter move, the quarterback must snap his head and shoulders back to playside to locate any quick slant or pinch move.

Scott Ertle, Stillwater Gazette

For our quarterback, the lead option is the easiest option for him to execute because it does not entail a fake of any kind.

- After counter steps, he attacks the inside shoulder of the defender to be optioned.
- If play is run away from our twins set, the quarterback must be quick to avoid being run down from the backside.

## Lead Back Assignments and Rules

- He counter steps away from playside. This two-step move entails an open step with the foot away from playside, and then a balance step with the opposite foot. When countering, he turns toward the line of scrimmage.
- During the first two steps, his head must be on a swivel, enabling the lead back to locate the defender responsible for pitch support.
- He sprints an arc path with his eyes focused on the man responsible for pitch support.
- He uses the same blocking techniques as in the lead option.

## Pitchback Assignments and Rules

- He executes a counter-step move away from playside. This two-step move is the same as the lead back.
- On the third step, he turns (toward the line of scrimmage) and sprints an arc path, staying in pitch phase with the quarterback.
- He follows the lead back as though he is making footprints in the snow.
- He should be prepared to turn upfield with the quarterback and be ready for a quick pitch.

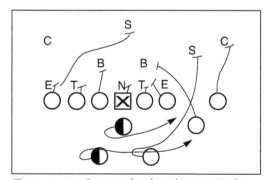

Figure 4-45. Counter lead option 52 Eagle

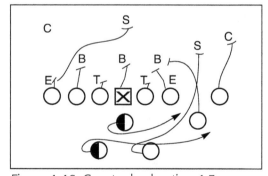

Figure 4-46. Counter lead option 4-3

# 5

# The Passing Attack

We are a ball-control, run-oriented offense, and our game plan is to move the football effectively on the ground against every opponent on our schedule. To complement our running game, the play-action pass was designed to take advantage of our smashmouth ground attack. Play-action allows the quarterback to sink a great inside fake to the dive back, duplicating the look of the dive-option series. While the defense is mandated to defend the run, the opportunity presents itself to take advantage of any weakness in an overly aggressive defensive unit.

## Play-Action Passing Game

The play-action series is an effective weapon at any point in the course of a game. Although proven to be particularly productive on first down, it is also very effective in short-yardage situations on second and third downs when the defenses are aligned to stop the run. In obvious passing situations, we will revert to our sprint-out scheme or our half-roll series to get the ball down the field.

The play-action series is designed to exploit the entire defensive secondary, but is deliberately limited by our staff to four basic combination routes. These routes are called: regular, jet, throwback, and flood. We also include verbal combinations such as curl-snake and post-snake if the situation warrants it. Along with these basic routes, we have included a single-screen pass to compensate for the overzealous rush of the defense. The footwork of the quarterback and dive back are slightly different than their footwork in the called dive and the dive option.

## Quarterback Assignments and Rules

- He opens with a long step playside at a 45-degree angle toward the dive back.
- He rides the dive back hip deep, guiding him into the B gap.
- He extends his arms and meshes with the dive tack three yards from the tip of the ball.
- He detaches at line of scrimmage, keeping his eyes downfield on the coverage.
- After detaching, he executes a three-step move straight back behind the offensive tackle. He should never get wider than the offensive tackle.
- *Note*: When going to the left, an additional adjustment step is necessary while rotating the hips.

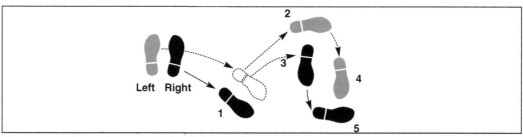

Figure 5-1. Play-action—quarterback footwork

## Dive Back Assignments and Rules

- His main responsibility is the onside linebacker.
- He open steps with the playside foot, as in the called dive.
- He meshes with the quarterback on his second step; his landmark is the B gap.
- He hugs the fake of the quarterback, while keeping his eyes glued on the linebacker.
- If the linebacker is blitzing, the dive back abandons the fake and blocks him; if no blitz, he makes a great fake, rolling over the ball, dipping the inside shoulder. If he is not tackled, he cuts back and stays out of the receivers' routes.

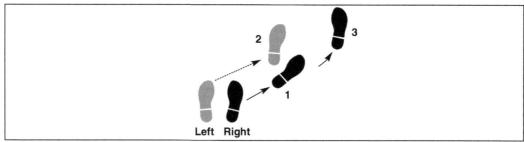

Figure 5-2. Play-action—dive back footwork

## Pitchback Assignments and Rules

- H open steps with the playside foot, as in the called dive.
- He takes a crossover step and continues parallel to line of scrimmage, staying in pitch phase.
- His key responsibility is any outside blitz from playside—backer or strong safety.
- If no blitz is imminent, he continues on a flair route.

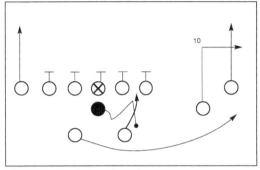
Figure 5-3. Play-action—jet

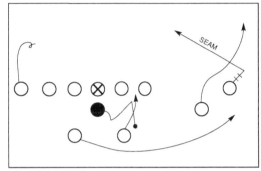
Figure 5-4. Play-action—regular

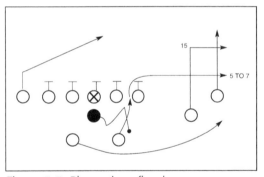
Figure 5-5. Play-action—flood

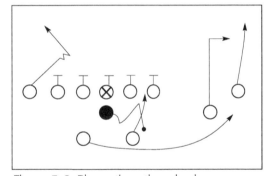
Figure 5-6. Play-action—throwback

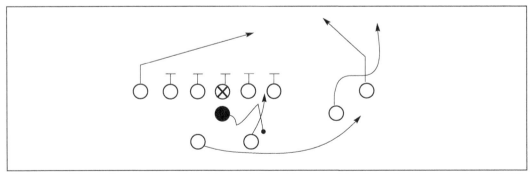
Figure 5-7. Play-action—post-snake, tight-end drag (Any combination of routes may be called.)

# Sprint-Out Passing Attack

The sprint-out passing attack is designed to take advantage of the type of athlete lined up at quarterback in the option offense. He is a good runner, and given the nature of the attack, he is conditioned to keep the ball and turn upfield as the ballcarrier when the opportunity presents itself. The sprint-out series keeps our quarterback on the move, allowing him to put pressure on the defensive perimeter with the option to run or pass the football. The flow helps to create seams and soft spots in the defensive secondary, affording easy reads for the quarterback.

## Quarterback Assignments and Rules

- Not a reverse pivot, his first step is an open step straight back with the playside foot, followed by two drive steps for depth.
- The third step aligns the quarterback on the hip of the tailback in the direction we are attacking
- His maximum depth is seven yards.
- Sprinting toward the sideline, he gets his shoulders around, squaring toward the target.
- If throwing, he runs through the target as a follow-through.

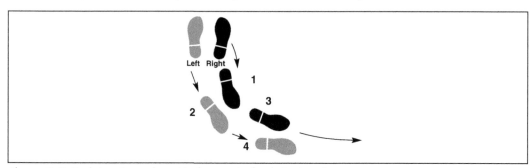

Figure 5-8. Sprint-out passing attack—quarterback footwork

## Lead Back Assignments and Rules

- He is responsible to block the third defender on the line of scrimmage.
- He open steps playside and sprints for a landmark one yard outside of 3's alignment.
- He blocks the defender head on, "to him and through him," and does not stop on contact.
- If 3 is blocked, he goes to the next level.

## Pitchback Assignments and Rules

- He sprints playside across the formation parallel to the line of scrimmage.

- Upon reaching a point outside the lead back's block, he turns upfield.
- He is responsible to block the first defender to show outside lead back's block.
- His blocking technique is identical to lead back's.
- If he has no one to block, he seals to the inside and remains alert for scraping linebackers.

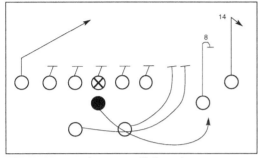

Figure 5-9. Sprint-out, roll, bench

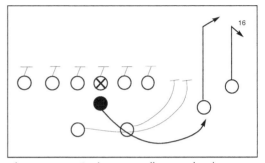

Figure 5-10. Sprint-out, roll, comeback

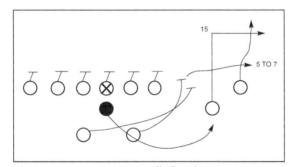

Figure 5-11. Sprint-out, roll, flood

# Half-Roll Passing Attack

Since we do not have a dropback scheme in our attack, the half-roll is a version of the dropback passing game. It is designed to give the quarterback ample time to get the ball downfield on the deeper routes and is employed most often in obvious passing situations. It fits nicely into the blocking scheme because it mirrors the blocking rules of our sprint-out series. The half-roll creates width and allows the quarterback to set up approximately six to seven yards behind the line of scrimmage. It also gives additional pass protection from the two running backs. We feel that, unlike the dropback series, the half-roll gives the quarterback greater mobility, while still allowing him more time to get the ball deep when necessary. It also affords flexibility in releasing the backs into the passing scheme and at the same time, sets up possibilities of the draw and our half-roll screen pass.

## Quarterback Assignments and Rules

- His first three steps are identical to the first three steps of the sprint-out series. His eyes are riveted on the coverage in the secondary.
- The fourth step is a plant, and then he makes adjustment steps to get into throwing position.
- He sets up six to seven yards deep, no wider than tackle-width, with ball in ready position and set to throw.

## Lead Back Assignments and Rules

- His first three steps are identical to the steps of the sprint-out series. He should keep eyes on the third outside defender.
- He sets up after the third step and is prepared to block 3 or any pass rush from the outside. He picks up inside seepage if necessary.
- He executes aggressive pass-block technique.

## Pitchback Assignments and Rules

- His first three steps are identical to the steps of the sprint-out series.
- He plants on the third step and turns to protect the backside pass rush.
- He executes aggressive pass-block technique. He should be alert for inside seepage.

Figures 5-12 through 5-17 illustrate a sample of the combination routes implemented in the half-roll passing game. The routes for the tight end include: drag, curl, throwback, post, and so on. The quarterback's throwing ability dictates the combination to concentrate on. A general rule for receivers in all of the passing schemes is that they will sprint through man coverage and will sit down in zone coverage.

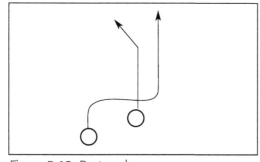

Figure 5-12. Post-snake

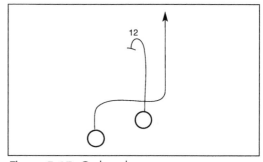

Figure 5-13. Curl-snake

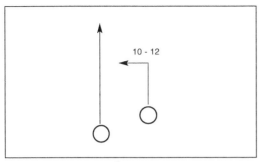

Figure 5-14. In-streak

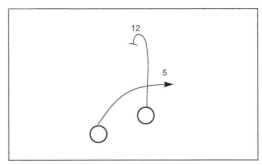

Figure 5-15. Curl-speed

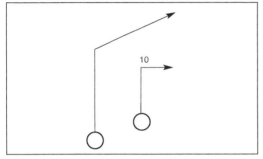

Figure 5-16. Out-corner

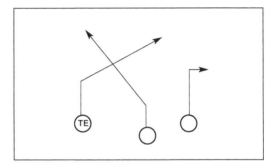

Figure 5-17. Out-cross

# Down-the-Line Series

The down-the-line series is a phase of the passing game that allows a team to take advantage of an aggressive defense with its secondary committed to stopping the option game. By its very nature, it is fast hitting, requiring an early read and a quick release by the quarterback. The quarterback must work close to the line of scrimmage, and timing is critical. The receivers have four routes in this series: flanker dump, flanker-dump roundup, tight-end dump, and whirley pass.

The quarterback works down the line of scrimmage, employing footwork identical to that of the lead option. It fits well into the blocking rules because it entails the same blocking scheme used in all of our options. The play is designed to mirror the option package, so defenses react quickly to defend the perimeter while aligning themselves to take away the pitch on the outside. The result creates an opportunity to exploit the secondary with dumps and quick release patterns.

## Quarterback Assignments and Rules

- Footwork is identical to the steps of the lead option, starting with a drop step with the backside foot.
- The second step is a balance step with the playside foot.

- On the third step, the quarterback will attack downhill toward the outside defender along the line of scrimmage.
- Before reaching tackle width, the quarterback will dump the ball to the flanker if he is open. The quarterback is reading the strong safety.
- If the flanker is covered, the quarterback will give ground, come under control, and look to his secondary receiver, the split end on a stop route.
- If everyone is covered, the quarterback will tuck the ball and get whatever he can straight ahead.

## Lead Back Assignments and Rules

- The lead back's responsibility is to aggressively block 3 on the defensive line of scrimmage.
- Footwork is identical to footwork on the lead option, except now he will block the man we normally option. The rule for the lead back on all dumps is that he is responsible for the third defender, and he must be occupied.

## Pitchback Assignments and Rules

- First three steps are identical to the lead option, but the pitchback has his head on a swivel, always aware of undue pressure from the backside.
- On the third step, the pitchback comes under control, and as in the half roll, he comes back and protects the backside. The first responsibility is the outside rush from the backside and then any seepage from inside.

*Flanker Dump*: With the flanker dump, the quarterback is keying the strong safety. If the strong safety comes up to defend the option, the quarterback will throw to the flanker. If the strong safety plays off to defend the pass, the quarterback will give ground and throw to the split end, who is running a seven-yard stop route.

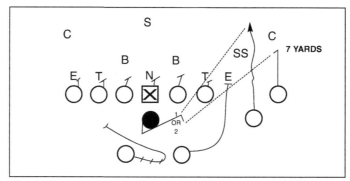

Figure 5-18. Down-the-line series—flanker dump

*Flanker-Dump Roundup*: The quarterback is keying the strong safety in the flanker-dump roundup, and if he comes up to defend the option, the quarterback will throw to the flanker on the roundup pattern. If the strong safety plays off, the quarterback will run the option. This play is the only dump where the pitchback does not block backside. *Note*: The defensive end is blocked by the lead back, so the option becomes a load option.

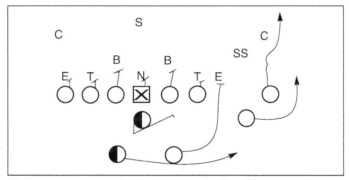

Figure 5-19. Down-the-line series—flanker-dump roundup

*Tight-End Dump*: We prefer to run the tight-end dump from our pro set, which gives a team two receivers to select from. The tight end executes an arc block as though he is option blocking. The quarterback keys the defender responsible for pitch support, and if the defender comes up to play the option, the quarterback will throw to the tight end. If the defender plays off, the quarterback will give ground and throw to the flanker, who will be running a seven-yard stop route.

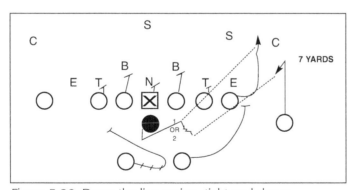

Figure 5-20. Down-the-line series—tight-end dump

*Whirley Pass*: The whirley pass is a deep pass and is particularly effective against a defense poised to stop the option. The combination routes preferred are the streak-post and the post-corner. The quarterback must sell the lead option so he plants at tackle-width, drops straight back, reads his key, and throws deep.

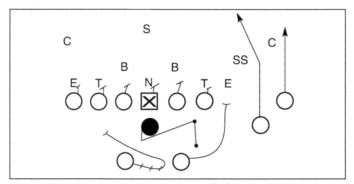

Figure 5-21. Down-the-line series—whirley pass

# Three-Step Passing Attack

The three-step passing game is a low-risk attack accompanied by a high percentage of completions. It is our quick game, and it creates an opportunity to get the ball into the hands of a talented receiver with greater frequency and consistency. The blocking rules governing the three-step are identical to the blocking rules of the play-action passing game. In keeping with a philosophy of simplicity, we have defined three patterns to perfect in this series. These include the slant, hitch, and fade. The three-step series fits very well into the audible system, and it is easily called at the line of scrimmage after the quarterback has made his pre-snap read.

In the huddle, the quarterback calls pro-right (or -left) quick pass. At the line of scrimmage, he notes the alignment of the secondary. With voice signals or hand signals, the quarterback directs the receivers as to the pattern they should run. When the quarterback and the receivers see that the defense is aligned in cover 2, it then becomes an automatic fade route for the receivers. They will execute a rip or swim technique to elude the bump corners.

*Note*: The footwork for the quarterback is different than the footwork involved in most three-step attacks. It does, however, mirror our option look.

## Quarterback Assignments and Rules

- The first step is a drop step with the foot opposite the quarterback's throwing arm.
- The second step is a balance step with the opposite foot.
- He makes an adjustment step to get into throwing position.
- The rhythm is one-two-step, gather, and throw.

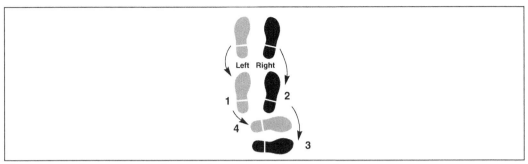

Figure 5-22. Three-step passing attack—quarterback footwork

## Running Backs Rule

• Backs will divide and step up to defend the outside rush.

*Pro-Right Quick Pass*: The pro-right quick pass is the call in the huddle. The team lines up in the formation called. The quarterback gets a pre-snap read of the defensive alignment and determines which of the three routes has the greatest probability of success. He then signals verbally or with hand signals to his receivers. If the quarterback does not like the defensive alignment, he may audible to a more suitable play.

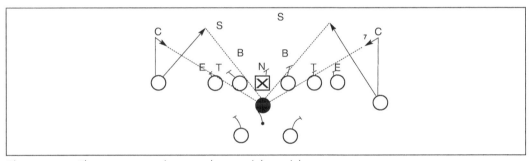

Figure 5-23. Three-step passing attack—pro-right quick pass

*Pro-Right Quick Pass Versus Cover 2*: In any cover-2 situation, the quarterback and the receivers will automatically execute the fade. Again, the quarterback may check to something altogether different.

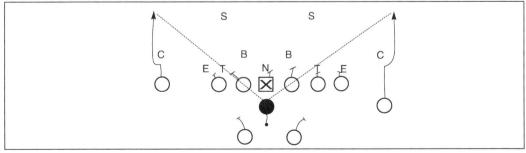

Figure 5-24. Three-step passing attack—pro-right quick pass versus cover 2

# Specialty Plays

The following special plays form an integral part of our total offensive package. They are discussed here for simplicity's sake, and they are not presented to the reader in any particular sequence or series. These plays are key to the success of our attack so they have been afforded the same attention and given equal time in our teaching scheme along with the rest of our playbook. The plays are not trick or gadget plays, and they meld nicely into the overall offensive plan.

## Roll Tight-End Screen

The tight-end screen play fits in well with our roll series and has been a big play for us over the years, particularly when we have the natural roll-type quarterback. It is a low-risk play and may be used throughout a game.

The footwork and backfield action mirror that of the roll series while the same blocking rules apply for the linemen. The exception of course, is with the guard and tackle on the screenside of the play. These players execute their initial steps, hit, jar, and then release, and form the screen outside of the tight end.

The quarterback rolls hard, getting his seven yards in depth and pulls up just beyond tackle width with a two-back lead. He will be looking to the twin receivers until he plants. If it is congested to the screenside, he will not risk the throw, but will instead pull the ball down and get what he can on the perimeter or straight ahead. The tight end will "invite" his man, then block him for a four count and release to a depth of at least four yards. Upon catching the football, the tight end will give a "go" call to alert his blockers. The play is equally effective from the twins set or the pro set.

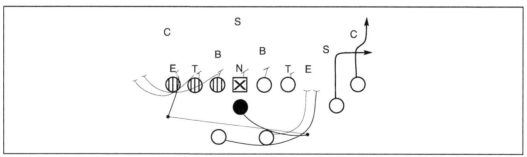

Figure 5-25. Roll tight-end screen

## Roll Draw

The roll draw is one of the most dynamic plays in this special package. It is a consistent ground gainer and has proven to be a game breaker. It is a low-risk play that pays off in big dividends. When in doubt, call the roll draw. Again, all of the action, footwork, and blocking rules mirror the roll series. Nothing changes for anyone except the lead back who is the ballcarrier. He will take his initial two steps and plant on his third step, and staying low, will form a pocket to receive the football.

The quarterback comes out hard, getting in the hip pocket of the pitchback, selling the roll, with his eyes downfield on the twins. The pitchback will turn up sharply to block the playside defensive end. The quarterback will mesh with the dive back between his second and third steps and deliver the ball. He will continue to roll outside, concealing the fact that he does not have the football. The dive back has no designated landmark, and he will read the blocks in front of him running to daylight.

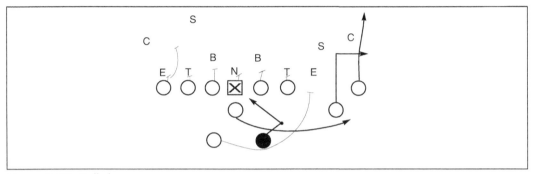

Figure 5-26. Roll draw

## Understreak

The understreak is a quick-hitting pass play from the play-action series. In the huddle, the quarterback calls pass right (or left) understreak, which tells the linemen that their blocking scheme is "big on big." The understreak is a quick release play and the backfield footwork and action is slightly altered.

The quarterback and playside dive back will execute the same footwork and technique as with the slant play. The dive back's landmark is the butt of the center. He is responsible for the fake and will abandon his landmark to block a plug linebacker if he sees him coming. The quarterback executes a drop step and balance step, while showing the football. The tight end executes an arc block and turns up on the corner as though blocking for the option, but instead of blocking, he will sprint past him. Simultaneously, the pitch back will run a wheel or flair route to the tight-end side of the formation.

The quarterback is keying the backside corner. If the corner stands or comes up to defend the option, he will throw to the tight end. If the corner backpedals, the quarterback will immediately throw to the pitchback, who most likely will have linebacker coverage from the inside.

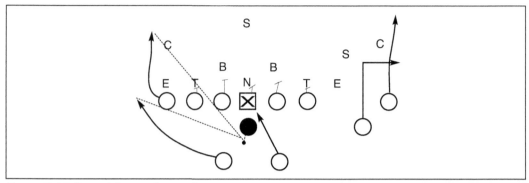

Figure 5-27. Pass right—understreak

## Half-Roll-Halfback Screen

The halfback screen from the half-roll series provides a play that is safe and easy to execute. It affords an opportunity to get the football out on the perimeter and into the hands of one of the best athletes. By its nature, the play creates flow in one direction while allowing for an attack in the other. Again, the linemen will execute the blocking scheme used in our half-roll series with the exception of the screenside guard and tackle. They will execute the same hit—the jolt and release technique used in the tight-end screen.

The pitchback will take his first three steps as though going into a full roll. On his third step, he will plant and come back to block the backside defensive end. He will invite the rush and block his man aggressively, releasing him to his outside shoulder. He will then get into his screen route and give a "go" call upon catching the ball.

The quarterback simply executes his normal footwork and technique employed in the half-roll series. He will look to the twin receivers and check to the backside to look for the pitchback on his route. If congested or covered, he will either unload out of bounds to the twins side of the field or will tuck it and run.

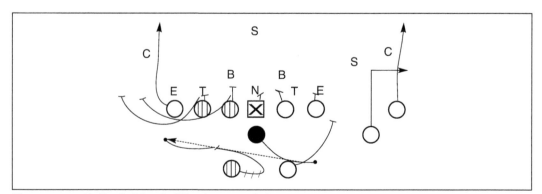

Figure 5-28. Half-roll right—half back screen left

## Three Pattern

The three pattern is a pass play that can be run from either the play-action series or the half-roll series. The play-action look is most effective when run on first or second down when the defense is playing the run. The play is also good in shorter yardage situations because of the good play fake involved.

In obvious passing situations, the half-roll technique gives a team more time to set up and allows for an opportunity to get the ball to one of the deep receivers. In either case, the call (pass right or half-roll right) will tell the linemen and the backs their blocking schemes and footwork techniques. This play is always run this from the pro set.

The quarterback will be reading a three-step progression with his receivers. The flanker will always run a deep post pattern while the split end runs a deep curl at 16 yards. The tight end drives off five yards, cuts sharply underneath, and then continues parallel to the line of scrimmage. He usually comes into the open at tackle width on the backside of the play.

The progression for the quarterback is to look to the post as he is executing his footwork for the play-action or the half-roll. If the post is open early, he will go there. If not, he reads the deep curl and the tight end coming underneath. The play is completed to the tight end in stride with ample running room after the catch.

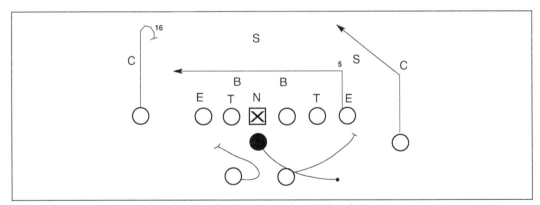

Figure 5-29. Pro right, half-roll right, three pattern (specialty play)

## Bootleg

The bootleg is a run-pass option for the quarterback and can be run from either the pro set or the twins formation. It is preferable to run it from the pro set because it gives an additional pass play from this set, and it also lends itself to a desired pattern. The footwork and action mirrors the isolation play.

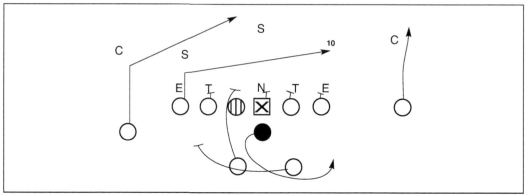

Figure 5-30. Bootleg

## Quick Screen

The quick screen is a low-risk play that allows a team to get the ball on the perimeter quickly. It is run from the play-action series, thus ensuring a good fake into the line to help set it up. The backfield action mirrors the dive and play-action series, while the line blocking is normal screen blocking. The flanker must drive hard off of the line of scrimmage to keep his defender on his heels or to get him to backpedal.

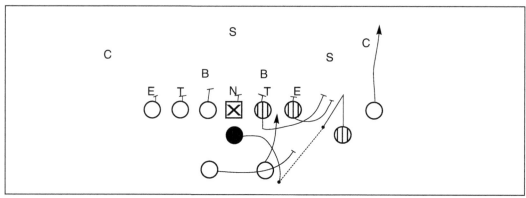

Figure 5-31. Quick screen right

## Automatics

We employ a number of automatics in our system. They are simple and intended to take advantage of any misalignment (intentional or not) by the opponent's defense. The wide receivers take note of the alignment of the defenders covering them, and if they observe any improprieties, they will then signal the quarterback, letting him know their intentions. For example, if the strong safety covering the flanker cheats too far to the inside, the flanker will hand signal to the quarterback that he is going to execute his dump route, while the split end does the same. The quarterback checks the free safety to be sure he cannot cover him from over the top. When satisfied, he executes the play on the "off-count" called in the huddle. Only the quarterback and the receivers have to know that you are running the automatic. If the quarterback happens to have the trap or the slant called, he will audible to something else to prevent the dive back from running into him. Time is not a factor because it is a quick stand-up-and-throw situation. We have scored from 80 yards out on this automatic.

The quarterback and center are always alert for the tap-and-go quarterback sneak when the opportunity presents itself. Lastly, our philosophy of "scratching where it itches" lends itself to taking advantage of what the defense gives us.

# Drills for Quarterbacks, Running Backs, and Receivers

Entire books are written covering a variety of drills that may be used in training offensive and defensive football players. The following examples are by no means a complete inventory of the drills available to the offensive coach, but they represent a series of related drills that we feel are pertinent in developing the competencies necessary to produce successful players at the skilled positions. Our daily routine of drills are related specifically to the game of football and to the positions mentioned previously. They involve throwing the ball, catching the ball, tucking, shifting, and protecting the ball, while sprinting and making subtle cuts.

After team calisthenics and stretching, players break off into groups with their respective position coaches. Backs and receivers line up four deep (in four or five groups, depending upon available numbers) on the chalk lines and go through the usual agility moves, including the high stepper, carioca, and 10-yard sprints, followed by what we simply call "ball drills." Drills are done daily and in both directions.

*Run Around the Hand (Left Hand-Right Hand)*: This drill improves agility and balance, quickness of feet, along with carrying, protecting, and shifting the football. From a two-point stance, the player at the front of the line will start with the football in the tuck position under the right arm. On the whistle, he will sprint five yards, plant the left hand, and run counter-clockwise 360 degrees. Coming up, he shifts the ball across his body, tucks it under his left arm, sprints forward five yards, plants his right hand, and runs clockwise 360 degrees. He finishes by sprinting the final five yards past the coach. The drill covers a total of 15 yards and is executed over and back.

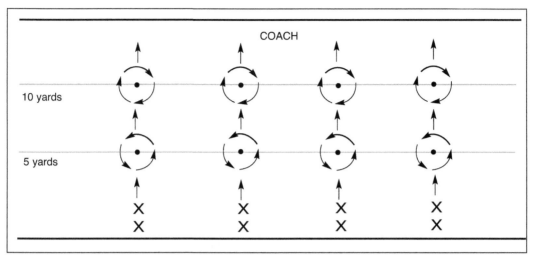

Figure 5-32. Run-around-the-hand drill

*Stumble Drill*: This drill will develop quickness and agility along with balance and recovery while carrying, shifting, and protecting the football. Starting from a two-point stance and with the ball in a tuck position under the right arm, the player steps out with his left foot, and while lunging forward, catches the full of his body weight with his left hand to keep from falling on his face. After his recovery, he will shift the ball across his body and tuck it securely under his left arm. While stepping quickly with his right foot and lunging forward, he catches his body weight with his right hand to keep from crashing. The procedure is repeated every other stride for a distance of 15 yards as quickly as possible. Through the years, this drill has paid off in big dividends during actual games. Running backs get tripped up and use the stumble principle to recover their balance and are able to get additional yardage. In some instances, it has enabled the ballcarrier to recover completely and go on to score. When breaking down game films, players are conditioned to watch for such occasions and are quick to yell, "Stumble drill."

*Fumble Drill*: This drill develops and improves hand quickness along with overall hand-eye coordination. On the whistle, player A at the front of the line sprints straight ahead. Player B tosses a "grounder" out in front of player A and gives him a ball call. At a full run, player A dips the near knee, scoops up the football, tucks it away, and sprints past the coach, who is 20 yards away. On the whistle, player A will then toss a "grounder" toward player B, who is sprinting straight ahead. He in turn scoops the ball, tucks it away, and sprints past the coach. The drill is done over and back.

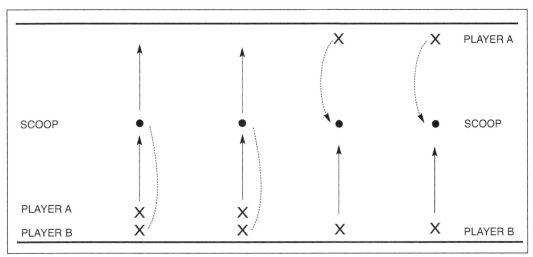

Figure 5-33. Fumble drill

*Passing and Receiving Drills*: Quarterbacks receive the snap from center and execute the proper footwork of our play-action pass series (both left and right). The coach will designate the route call. The routes include the out, in, curl, short post, and short corner. Generally, three routes are employed in this drill during any given practice period. Quarterbacks alternate calling cadence. The drill stresses footwork, disciplined routes, throwing, catching, tucking, and protecting the football.

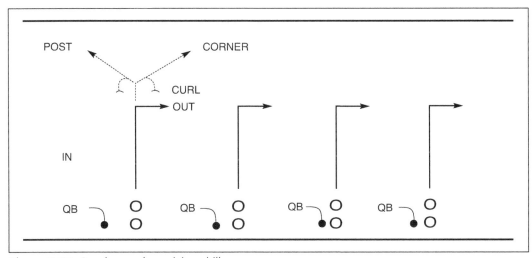

Figure 5-34. Passing and receiving drills

*Left Shoulder-Right Shoulder*: Quarterbacks will move out in front of their groups 10 yards off. The player at the front of the line faces away from the quarterback and assumes a good athletic stance. When the quarterback yells "Ready," the receiver foot-fires, and when he hears "Left shoulder," he drives his left elbow through, turning his body 180 degrees toward the quarterback. The quarterback delivers the ball face-high as the receiver turns. The receiver must locate the ball, catch it (thumbs down above the midriff, and thumbs up below the midriff), and then look it into the tuck position. The drill is repeated until each player has had the opportunity to catch the ball both to the left and to the right.

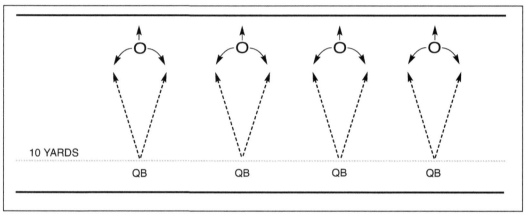

Figure 5-35. Left shoulder-right shoulder drill

*Break Right-Break Left*: This drill emphasizes coming under control, breaking down, making sharp cuts, catching the football, tucking it away, and turning sharply upfield. The quarterbacks face their group and are off 20 yards. Receivers go on the quarterback's command. The drill is done over and back.

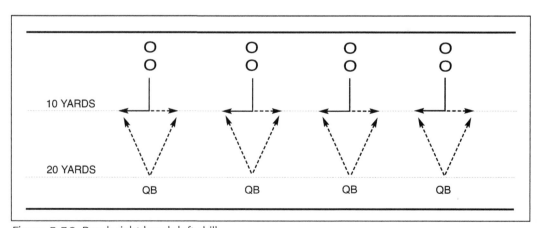

Figure 5-36. Break right-break left drill

*Pass-Repass*: The quarterback faces his group from 15 yards off. On his command, the receiver will sprint straight ahead. The quarterback throws to the oncoming receiver, who in turn tosses it back to the quarterback as he sprints past him. The quarterback will allow the receiver to get down the field and then launches a deep, over-the-shoulder-type pass to him, while giving him a ball call. The receiver will make the catch, tuck the ball away, and sprint to the end zone. This drill is great to build the receiver's confidence in making the difficult, over-the-shoulder catch.

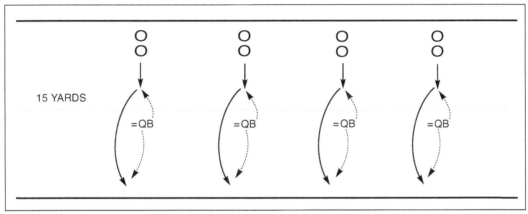

Figure 5-37. Pass-repass drill

# 6

# Blocking With the Offensive Line

Offensive linemen, or the "jumbos," are often second bananas. They go unnoticed until a block is missed and an offense stalls. Other than their immediate family, only the coaches and devout football purists are likely to observe and appreciate their exploits.

## Player Selection

Through the years, we have been blessed with terrific offensive lines that resulted in an offensive scheme that was consistent. We have yet to see a championship team at any level that isn't strong in this department. Remember that old ad about Maytag repairmen being the loneliest people in the world? On any level of competition, offensive linemen receive the least praise. But who is more essential to a team's success?

We run the same plays as most veer teams, including the hard dive, option, outside veer, lead option, counters, and cutbacks. We have learned from experience that the most important yard in football is the one that separates the offensive and defensive lines. The offensive line requires players who can gain and maintain control of that magic yard for the veer to be most effective. It is important that we are strong at the point of attack, able to stop penetration, and cut off pursuit. It takes a good athlete to accomplish those things, and we remind them of their importance daily.

The size and strength of today's jumbos is the biggest change in high school football in the last 20 years. Add the fact that they have more liberal rules in pass blocking, and you have a whole new ball game. Kids don't play backyard football with the intent of someday being referred to as a "hog" or some other affectionate name. They will realize soon enough that they are expected to have heavy contact on every play and spend most of their time bent over.

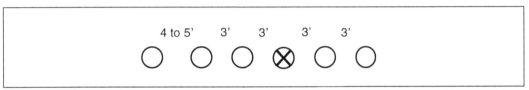

Figure 6-1. Line spacing

## Assignments

*Tackles*: We like to put our bigger players here, including those duffel-bag types. We put our best one-on-one blocker at left tackle to force us to call more plays to the left for balance. The defense usually puts their best player on the opposite side; therefore, you gain an advantage at the onset by running left. They take their split one yard from the guard's near foot

*Guards*: We can get by with smaller players for guards because the block wouldn't have to be held as long to get our quarterback free to move down the line. Our guards and tackles are interchangeable and that gives us more depth, which is a huge plus. They take a split one yard from the center's near foot.

*Center*: We would like to have a solid blocker who can work upfield, but quick hands are the most important asset. We have won several games because our opponent's center was slow snapping the ball. At the first practice each fall, we line up our linemen and have them snap to each quarterback. The one with the quickest hands gets the call, and we will teach him how to block later. Speed kills.

*Tight End*: We like a tackle-type player who can catch a football. If we have to choose, then we want an aggressive blocker for the outside veer play. Tight ends take a split of at least four feet from the near foot of the tackle.

# Stance

We teach our linemen to use a four-point stance with the butt high, as if they're getting ready to run the 100-meter dash. We have found that it keeps them lower and gets them off the ball quicker. It's also a much easier technique to teach. We do a lot of short sprint work, and the four-point stance makes those big guys feel like college sprinters. Quickness is the most important feature of this stance that we settled on and perfected.

Linemen should slightly stagger their feet with the strong foot forward. They should keep their feet under the armpits and not get any wider. They should place the hands in front as if getting ready to run a sprint at the Olympic games. This position may seem awkward because they cannot raise their head to check defensive alignment, but our blocking technique makes that a moot point.

Figure 6-2. Stance

# Offensive Linemen Traits

- *Smarts*: Linemen must be able to understand the concept of each play. Offensive linemen tend to be better students as a rule and tend to be more orderly.
- *Strength*: Players must be strong enough to sustain a block and not get overpowered by a defensive lineman. To develop such strength, the power clean or clean and jerk may be more beneficial lifts than a bench press. Strong thighs and lower-back strength are essential. Power is to an offensive lineman what quick feet and skating ability are to a hockey player.
- *Desire*: Offensive lineman take pride in carrying out their assignments on every play while never taking a lazy step. They must have the ability to go all out from snap to whistle.
- *Thick Skin*: This position demands perfection of technique—practices and drills should be intense. Players must be made to realize that criticism is directed at what they do and not who they are.
- *Good Feet*: Jumbos must have the ability to move their feet while maintaining control of the defender. Balance depends on mastery of footwork technique. Although speed is not required, quickness is essential.

Figure 6-3. Offensive line with correct splits

# Offensive Line Play

Every line candidate wants to play defense, so motivation is seldom a problem when selecting players for that unit. However, it can be a different story when it comes to offense. At every practice, we remind our offensive linemen that they are the "skilled players" on our team.

We like to place our larger linemen on offense because they tend to create larger running lanes based just on their girth, so we do look at size even before quickness. Size is impossible to develop once practice starts, but quickness can be improved with each daily practice. We realize that every team has a lot of small, hardnosed, tough linemen, but for our money, size is the most essential quality (within reason). The veer offense doesn't require outrageously huge offensive lines to control the ball.

Toughness and strength are also important factors in selecting offensive linemen. The winners of our one-on-one blocking drill will find themselves on the offensive side of the ball. We are firm believers in tough defenses, as our record has shown, but not at the expense of the offensive line. The defensive lineman has a lot of things to help, such as stunts—and, if he is a free spirit, he can hide his sins with aggressive play. It's harder to block than pursue.

We are tough on our offensive linemen, but we explain our reasons to them prior to the season. They must be disciplined to the point that every move becomes automatic. They must have thick skin, but at the same time, they must be rewarded to gain confidence and esteem. The media and fans will not recognize their efforts— therefore, the coaches and team must.

Sometimes, you have another problem that must be overcome. Many jumbos have been taught all their lives to take it easy on the little guys, so they develop a more gentle nature growing up. If they didn't, there wouldn't be any little guys.

# Drill Philosophy

Most of our drills are aimed at improving quickness because we believe that it is essential and can be developed. If we had to pick one drill that does the most to enhance quickness, it would be team takeoff, with the entire offensive team running a selected play. Players sprint hard for 20 meters and are stopped with a whistle. We see how many times we can take off in a 10-minute period.

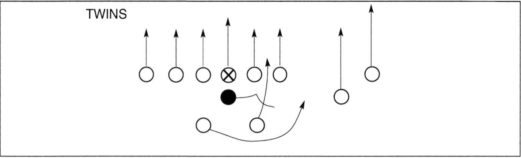

Figure 6-4. Team takeoff drill

During the drills, the coach calls the position or name of players who are the slowest off the ball. We go hard for 20 minutes at every practice. Doing so dramatically improves the overall quickness and execution of the squad. All plays and drills start with a snap and end with a whistle. If they pull up short before the end of the play or drill, they are learning a bad habit in practice. We drill over and over that the play starts with the snap and ends with a whistle. Most of our drill time is spent in the chutes and flying out while blocking a handheld shield, team takeoff, and team skills. Every drill that we perform is directly related to an actual game situation. In other words, we don't run drills for the sake of the drill, but for its ability to prepare players for actual play situations.

# Technique

In our version of the veer, the interior linemen have two basic blocks to power the running game: the zone block and the backside scoop. The initial moves are the same, but the points of attack differ.

## Zone Block—Playside Block

The lineman explodes off the line of scrimmage and places hitting triangle (forehead and forearms with elbows out) in the defensive player's outside armpit. He swings his butt and outside leg around his opponent and works upfield by putting pressure on him from outside in. He should run the 100-meter dash through his outside breast and make sure that the opponent does not get into pursuit path.

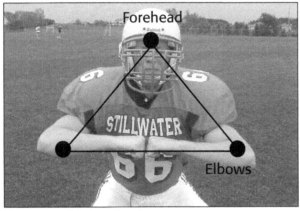

Figure 6-5. Hitting triangle

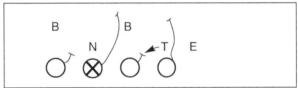

Figure 6-6. Zone blocking scheme (with emphasis on working upfield)

Figure 6-7. Zone block

# Blocking

We call our man-to-man block a "base block" for this book; however, our players call it a "horse block." This block is practiced daily, and our players get a fit and walk through the block several times prior to practice. The base (horse) block consists of the lineman placing the hitting triangle (forehead and elbows form the triangle) into the defender's outside breast or armpit. The lineman should work his head and shoulders upfield and pinch his head on the defender's outside armpit as if he is biting into the defender's "pecs." This block is easy to coach and is the father of the "reach" and "fan" blocks that we often use.

Figure A. Base block

We don't slow the offensive linemen down with a lot of complicated blocking rules. We let them sprint off the ball and get after people. We do assign a block to a specific defender, but only at the point of attack, and the aiming point is the outside breast. This approach allows the offensive player to block the looping or slanting defensive lineman. Since our running back moves opposite his block, he is never wrong if he gets off the ball and fires into the defender. If our blocker has an inside or outside aiming point, we give him help from another lineman, which produces automatic combos without making a line call. Our blocker comes off hard at his aiming point. If it's not there, he continues on his path to levels 2 and 3.

We will not attempt to cover tackling because it doesn't fall under the offensive option scheme, but we do spend some time in this area in case the defense gets a pick or scoops a fumble. On a pass play, the quarterback follows his pass and all others sprint to the ball. The passer must get himself into position to prevent a long return of a fumble or interception and basically "save the bacon."

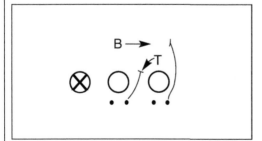

Figure B. Zone technique versus slant tackle

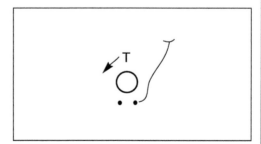

Figure C. Slant tackle technique

## Scoop Block

We use this block on the side away from the play that is called. The offensive lineman explodes with playside foot into the gap and keeps his outside arm free to ward off the defensive lineman. He maintains pressure to the playside and cuts off pursuit. We feel our line must master these basics for us to consistently move the ball on the ground. The most important aspect of the block is the takeoff. Good blocking technique and a thorough understanding of the blocking rules are next in the order of importance. When teaching, we break the blocks into: takeoff, contact, lock-on, and follow-through. Players walk through all phases of the block with the coach talking them through the steps.

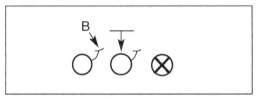

Figure 6-8. Backside scoop block

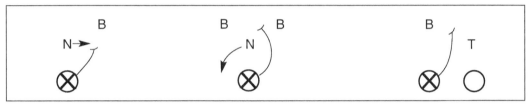

Figure 6-9. Coaching points of zone block—center

We scoop the backside pursuit on all of our running plays. The block is executed by taking a 45-degree step toward the playside gap. A first step of six inches will put us into position to read whether a defensive lineman is stunting toward us, or if we accelerate to the next level. On 98 percent of our running plays, the assignments are kept simple. In other words, if you can count to three, you can learn your running play assignments.

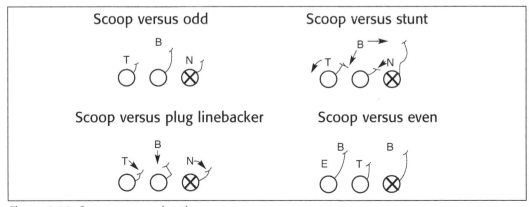

Figure 6-10. Scoop versus situations

Figure 6-11. Scoop block

# Counting Defenses

In 98 percent of our running plays, we zone block playside and scoop block backside. We assign defenders to our linemen by counting the defense. The number 0 is assigned to the center, with 1 assigned to the guards, and so on.

*Center*: Blocks 0, steps hard playside, eyeballs for slant tackle or stunting linebacker.
*On Guard*: Blocks 1, steps hard playside, looks for slant tackle or plug linebacker.
*On Tackle*: Blocks 2, steps hard and blocks through outside breast. If tackle slants inside, he stays locked on for automatic double-team with the on guard.
*Off Guard*: Blocks 1, replaces the feet of the center. If the noseguard slants toward him, he blocks the nose. Note: By replacing the feet of the center, he is taking away their inside blitzing.
*Off Tackle*: Blocks 2, steps hard to playside gap. If nothing appears, then he heads for the free safety. He does not go around if defender gets in his way—then he knocks him into a pile.

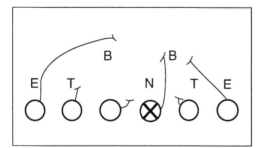

Figure 6-12. Blocking scheme versus 5-2

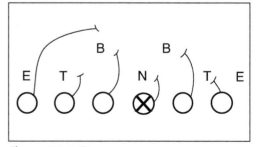

Figure 6-13. Zone—scoop

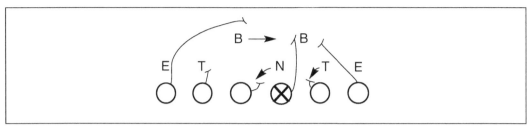

Figure 6-14. Blocking scheme versus—5 stunt

It is important to make sure that the linemen understand that they must sustain their blocks from snap to whistle. They cannot pull up short or take lazy steps. We like to remind our players that a high school football game lasts 48 minutes, however, when you consider the time spent getting into the huddle, in the huddle, coming out of the huddle, and putting the ball in play—you have approximately 12 minutes of action. So, 12 minutes of action in a 48-minute contest means only six or seven minutes on offense and the same on defense if you platoon 12 to 13 minutes for your two-way iron men. Each play lasts only about four to six seconds. Asking them to go all out for four to six seconds per play for a total of 6 or 12 minutes, with a rest in between each play is not an impossible demand. Everyone must hustle 100 percent of the time. It isn't like basketball or hockey, with non-stop action while the clock is ticking.

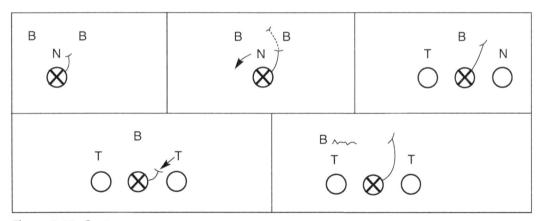

Figure 6-15. Center—zone

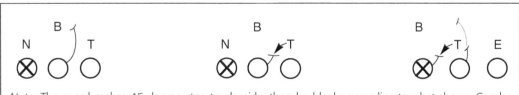

Note: The guard makes 45-degree step to playside, then he blocks according to what shows. Combo blocks become automatic if required.

Figure 6-16. Guard—zone

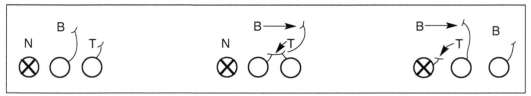

Figure 6-17. Tackle–zone

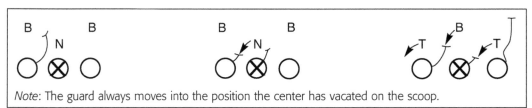

*Note*: The guard always moves into the position the center has vacated on the scoop.

Figure 6-18. Guard–scoop

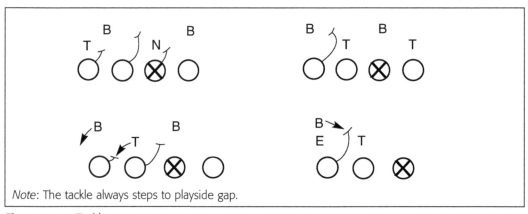

*Note*: The tackle always steps to playside gap.

Figure 6-19. Tackle–scoop

# Blocking

### Zone Blocking

Th linemen explode off the line of scrimmage on the proper angle while ripping through the playside gap. Each lineman should step and assume that a defender will occupy that gap. He takes a short jab step with his near foot and places the hitting triangle to the defender's outside breast and works upfield.

### Combo Blocking

The combo block is automatic in our scheme whenever we encounter a stunt or a stack that presents a problem for the blocker. *Note*: Remember that all combo blocks are automatic and do not require a line call. Why confuse things? The defense will determine the technique that you will use. You can achieve maximum takeoff by your linemen due to the simplicity of assignments.

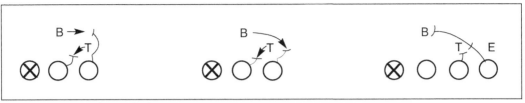

Figure 6-20. Combo technique

Figure 6-21. Over technique

## Reach Block

The offensive lineman attacks the outside knee and thigh of his opponent. When he gets there, he should reach up, "bite the cheek" of the defensive man (i.e., punch his head toward the defender's butt), and then sprint 100 yards downfield.

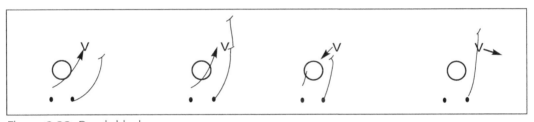

Figure 6-22. Reach block

## Work Upfield

We stress that our linemen block each level before moving upfield. The worst thing that a lineman can do is miss his line-of-scrimmage block, and then turn and chase a defender into his backfield.

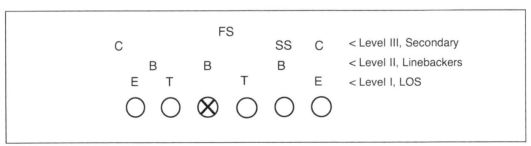

Figure 6-23. Work upfield

If a block is lost, the blocker should accelerate to the next level and block something. A lineman who chases a defender after a missed block will get in the way of his backs and create more havoc. An offensive lineman must *never* chase a defender into the backfield.

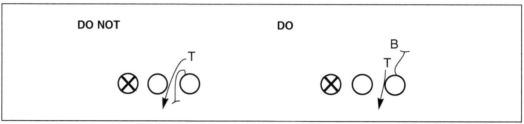

Figure 6-24. Reacting to a missed block

## Tight End Arc Block

Most blocks executed by the tight end require an arc block on playside option plays (except a lead option). He will zone, scoop, and operate out of the same stance as interior linemen. The tight end should block high and make himself as big as possible. He should get close enough to step on the defender's toes before setting his block, then drop his butt at first contact and run through defender.

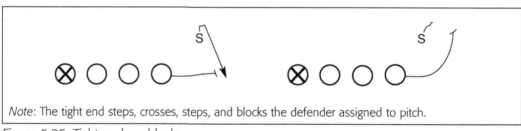

*Note:* The tight end steps, crosses, steps, and blocks the defender assigned to pitch.

Figure 6-25. Tight end arc block

## Tight End Veer Block

The tight end blocks heavily to the inside on the outside veer and lead option plays. He is to block the first linebacker to his inside on both plays. If anything is shaded on the outside of playside tackle, he runs through it.

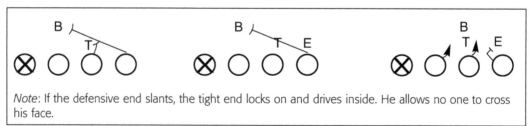

*Note:* If the defensive end slants, the tight end locks on and drives inside. He allows no one to cross his face.

Figure 6-26. Tight end veer block

## Tight End Blocking Scheme

The ideal tight end in the veer would be strong enough to block solid in man-to-man situations, quick enough to block or seal linebackers, and agile enough to block defensive backs. As mentioned previously, he would be a cross between a tackle and a split end. The tight end's stance is identical to that of the interior offensive lineman. The tight end never should allow the defense to have a stack on him (Figure 6-26). On a few occasions, our tight ends move a stack as much as five yards outside our tackle (Figure 6-27). The same rules would apply to the tackle if he is the end man on the line of scrimmage (Figure 6-28).

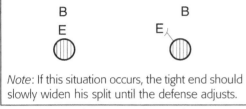

*Note*: If this situation occurs, the tight end should slowly widen his split until the defense adjusts.

Figure 6-27. Adjusting to the stack

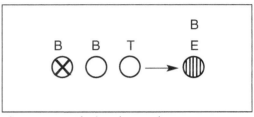

Figure 6-28. Flexing the stack

Figure 6-29. Flexing the tackle

When the tight end is on the offside of a called play, he executes a crossfield technique (Figure 6-29). He tries to get to a level-2 or level-3 block at the point of attack. The tight end will arc release on all options called to his side except on the lead option (Figure 6-30). The defensive lineman on the tight end jams him, thus keeping him from releasing inside (Figure 6-31). This jam would occur on the outside veer, lead option for the tight end, and any play where the on tackle is the end man on the line of scrimmage. In this event, we would use our slip block.

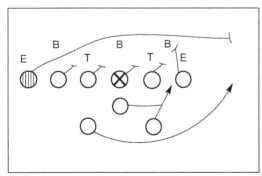

Figure 6-30. Tight end crossfield

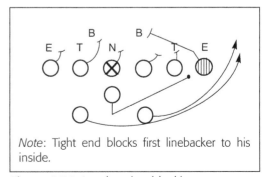

*Note*: Tight end blocks first linebacker to his inside.

Figure 6-31. Lead option blocking

*Note*: Defensive player controls the tight end while maintaining outside control.

Figure 6-32. Defensive end jams

## Tight End Slip Block

The tight end steps flat down the line on his first step with the inside foot, then executes a crossover step with the outside foot while twisting at the trunk to get free from defender and regain course to block. When a tight end blocks inside, we teach him to step down flat with his inside foot, cross over with his outside foot, and then rip up and through the defensive player (similar to a slant technique of a defensive lineman). The slip block has been a tremendous technique for us. It enables the tight end or on tackle to move inside without being tied up by the defensive end (end defender on the line of scrimmage).

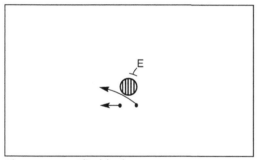

Figure 6-33. Slip block

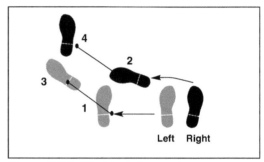

Figure 6-34. Slip block footwork

The slip block works well and the technique is easy to master. This technique can be used often by the tight end on the block required for the outside veer. The on tackle toward the splitside on any option would use this block if getting pressure from an outside defender.

Figure 6-35. On tackle using slip block

# Running Game

We have a simple numbering system that requires that our linemen only need to count to three. Our center is assigned to the 0, our guards to 1, our tackles to 2, and on rare occasions, our tight end is assigned 3. If a player can count to three, then he knows every offensive line assignment, which enables him to get off the ball with a quick release and concentrate on blocking technique. Note: The defense can throw a ton of defensive sets at you, but with zone-scoop blocking, it becomes a moot point. Remember to count defenders inside out.

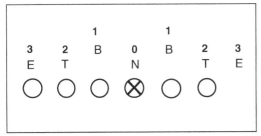

Figure 6-36. Offensive line assignments versus 5-2

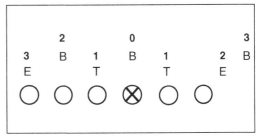

Figure 6-37. Offensive line assignments versus 4-3

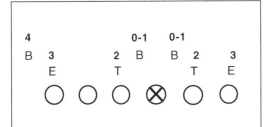

Figure 6-38. Offensive line assignments versus split

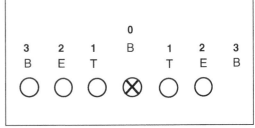

Figure 6-39. Offensive line assignments versus 6-1

# Drills

We emphasize that the offensive lineman's first step should be outward and never upward. This placement is aided by our unique four-point stance with feet under the armpits, butt high, and hands about nine inches in front of the knees. In other words, just tell them to assume a sprinter's stance as if they were in the finals of the 100-meter dash at the Olympic games.

*Stance Starts*: Set stance—Have them explode out of their stance and sprint 10 yards, hard and fast repeatedly for five minutes.
*Carioca*: The carioca will help to develop quick feet and have players tighten their footwork until they slowly advance.

*Crab With Butt Roll*: This drill checks agility and gets them thinking about getting back to a hitting position.

*Blocking Fit*: The player walks from his stance and places his hitting triangle in defender's playside breast. Then, he drives them as the opponent shifts directions, forcing the blocker to adjust to the defender to maintain a block. We picked this drill up at a camp at the University of Wisconsin, and it has been golden for us.

*Chutes*: Most of our drill time is spent in the chutes. This area is great to develop stance, takeoff and blocking techniques. Our shop and grounds crew built several chutes that have three stalls per unit.

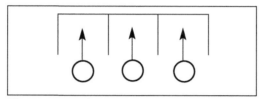

Figure 6-40. Chutes

We start off with stance-starts, calling out the names of the quicker players. We progress with the players blocking on handheld shields at the end of the chutes. We move the blockers further into the chute so they have a shorter distance to strike a dominant blow. We concentrate on blocking technique and hitting force. Several times, we will have them shout, "Outward, never upward." We will spend at least 25 minutes daily on this drill, Monday through Wednesday.

Figure 6-41. Starts on a snap…

Figure 6-42. …ends on a whistle.

**Off on the Ball Drill**

*Equipment Needed*: Six stand-up dummies, two footballs

*Description*: Place the entire offensive line in the set position with the dummies stationed five yards away (additional offensive lines should be ready for their turn). On the cadence count, the offensive line should move out and apply the base block technique to the dummies.

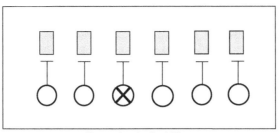

Figure 6-43. Off on the ball drill

## Assignment Drill

*Equipment Needed*: Six stand-up dummies, two footballs
*Description*: Place various defensive sets against an entire offensive line. On the cadence count, the offensive line should move out, each lineman blocking the proper defensive man with correct technique.

# Veer Offense Philosophy

The veer offense, with our scheme of pass and run blocking, is simple if you can count to three. This simplicity enables the linemen to concentrate on quickness off the ball and on blocking techniques. We ask our linemen to run short sprints in bursts of five to six seconds, and we end every play or drill rep with a whistle. To test a lineman by making him run a mile within a certain time is cruel, especially for the jumbos. All summer, that young man is miserable just thinking about running that mile in front of the team. If he wanted to run, he would have joined the cross-country team. Distance running is as important to line play as golf clubs are to fly-fishing.

We use few plays and even fewer blocking schemes. Essentially the same blocking is used on 90 percent of our plays. Obviously, this approach allows us to master our technique to a greater degree, have fewer mental errors, and get more repetitions during our practices. We feel that this is the secret to good execution. We always have had lines that were quick off the ball, incurred few penalties, and were well disciplined. Running backs will become hard-nosed if they have confidence in their offensive line. Our guards and tackles become interchangeable, which provides greater depth.

Our base plays are the hard dive and the outside veer. As on most of our plays, we zone block on the playside (onside) and scoop the backside (offside). Our linemen use a four-point stance, similar to the starting stance of a sprinter at a track meet. The tail is lifted, with feet under the armpits (narrower than most teams' stances) and eyes up. We tell our linemen that they are to take off along their path as if running a 100-meter dash. Much of our practice time is spent working on this, and we feel the limited number of techniques we use contributes to our success.

For recognition and communication purposes, we count the defensive personnel. A man over our center is the 0, the first defensive player to each side is 1, the second defensive player to each side is 2, and so on. The off guard always replaces the feet of the center—the law of the jungle.

However, because we primarily use zone and scoop blocking principles, our linemen are usually blocking through their playside gap. Defensive slants and stunts may cause changes in who a lineman blocks. Therefore, we often are more concerned with where a defensive player is than who a defensive player is.

## LINE BLOCKING IN THE PASSING GAME

Our veer attack includes four passing schemes:
- Dump passes
- Screens
- Play-action
- Sprint-out

## Dump Passes

This quick, play-action pass can be thrown from all option plays. The line blocks as if it is a running play because the action and release are so quick that the linemen are not in danger of being downfield. The dump pass is used to keep the fast-pitch support team from cheating and jumping on the option plays. Interior linemen will zone and scoop as they would in a running play when we call any type of dump pass. We want to influence the playside linebacker, so we must fire out aggressively. At the point when the tight end clears, the ball will be delivered. Remember, in this offense, the players must sell all pass plays as a run. If the dump is covered, a potential option run is still alive. Linemen must not assume that it is always going to be a pass. It's a good play coming back to the single tight-end side, but can also be run effectively from the pro. This technique will force the defensive secondary to tip its hand early if they are in zone coverage. The action will be the same for the interior line on all dump passes (tight end, frontside linebacker, and split end).

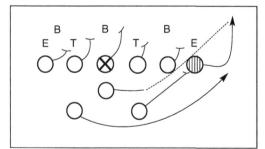

Figure 6-44. Tight-end dump versus 4-3

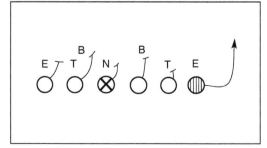

Figure 6-45. Tight end dump versus 5-2 Eagle

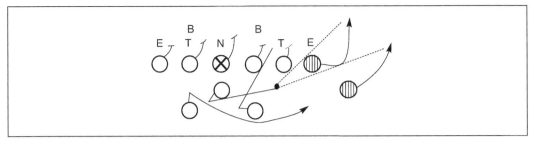

Figure 6-46. Counter tight end dump

# Screens

### Tight-End Screen

The tight end drives hard downfield for three yards, plants his foot, and moves back toward the ball.

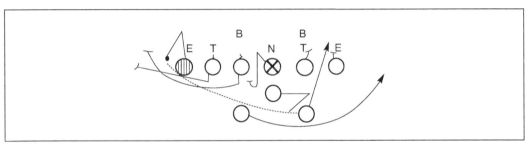

Figure 6-47. Tight-end screen

*On Tackle*: Blocks with hit, jolts, releases and blocks the widest defender on the field.
*On Guard*: Hits, jolts, releases, and blocks the first defender inside the tackle's block.
*Center*: Seals to playside.
*Off Guard and Tackle*: Zone blocks and sells misdirection.

### Quick Screen

When the linebackers and defensive backs start to quick flow, the quick screen becomes a good way to get the ball into the hands of the team's burner.

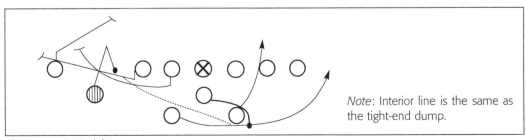

*Note*: Interior line is the same as the tight-end dump.

Figure 6-48. Quick screen

# Play-Action

We make the defenders think run and keep the linebackers out of pass coverage. Linemen will fan block the playside and man block the backside.

Figure 6-49. Fan playside, man backside

*Fan Block:* On guard blocks first down lineman on playside. On tackle blocks second down lineman on playside.

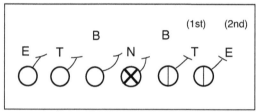

Figure 6-50. Fan versus 5-2

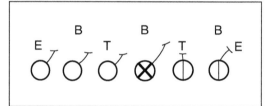

Figure 6-51. Fan versus 4-3

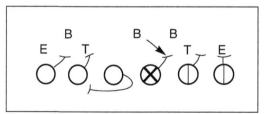

Figure 6-52. Fan versus split 6

## Assignments for All Play-Action Passes

*Tight End*: Blocks 3 or pattern.
*On Tackle*: Blocks second down lineman.
*On Guard*: Blocks first down lineman.
*Center*: Blocks man, off linebacker, backdoor.

*Note*: Whenever a lineman hears the call as pass right or left, he knows his assignment.

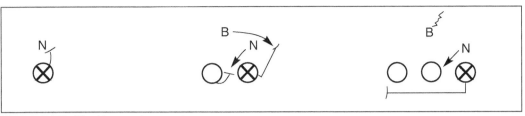

Figure 6-53. Blocking assignments

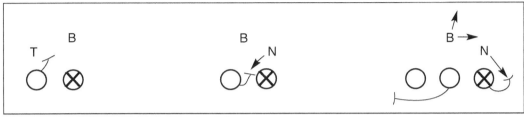

Figure 6-54. Off guard blocks 1 or backdoor

Figure 6-55. Off tackle blocks 2

# Sprint-Out

The sprint-out pass puts pressure on the outside containment people and gives the quarterback a good view of the field. As in play-action, we like to use combination patterns with our split ends and flankers.

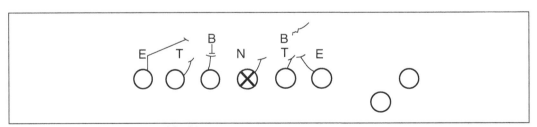

Figure 6-56. Sprint-out pass blocking

*Linemen*: Block man on the line of scrimmage over you. If man over is a linebacker, then check to make sure he does not plug. If linebacker goes to cover, help next blocker inside. Note: Block man unless he is a linebacker. If backer goes to cover, then block next man inside. If backer comes, then block him solid.

# Pass Blocking Summary

*Dump Pass*: Option blocking. Zone playside, scoop backside, treat as a run.

*Screen Pass*:

- On tackle—Block with hit, jolt, release and block widest defender on the field.
- On guard—Hit, jolt release, and block first defender inside of the Tackle's block.
- Center—Blocks 1.

*Play-Action*: Onside use fan block, offside use man. It doesn't get easier!

*Sprint-Out*: Block man on; if man on is a linebacker, then block if he comes. If not, help next lineman to the inside.

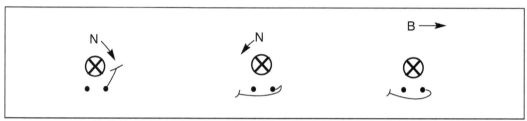

Figure 6-57. Center assignment in play-action pass

# Line Drills to Develop Zone and Scoop Techniques

### One-on-One Blocking Drill

*Equipment Needed*: None

*Description*: The defensive player assumes defensive position over the center, rotates to position over defensive lineman, assumes defensive line position, and/or rotates to the end of the line. The offensive blocker takes the defender any way he can and stays locked on until the coach blows the whistle.

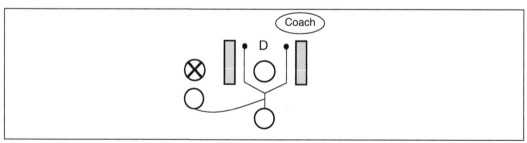

Figure 6-58. One-on-one blocking (heavy contact)

*Benefits*:

- Simulates game-type situation.
- Excellent contact drill for centers. They trade off among themselves after four or five reps.

- Isolates the one-on-one aspects of blocking.
- Helps coaches determine the best line position for each player.
- The coaches can see who the heavy hitters are.
- Preps defensive types to read movement of man or ball and shed blocker.
- Identifies backs and wide receivers who are willing to run hard into the hot zone.

## Footwork Blocking Drill

*Equipment Needed*: Hand shields
*Description*: Defenders hold shields and the blockers are forced to react to a situation according to what they encounter. Example situations are shown in Figures 6-59 through 6-61. We work these situations every day in practice so that the lineman's reactions will become automatic. They are reinforced every time a play is run during team scheme. We create the same type of practice drill situations for our passing game. We always place a defender over our center in practice to make him snap and step hard to playside, ready to block and work his head and shoulders upfield.

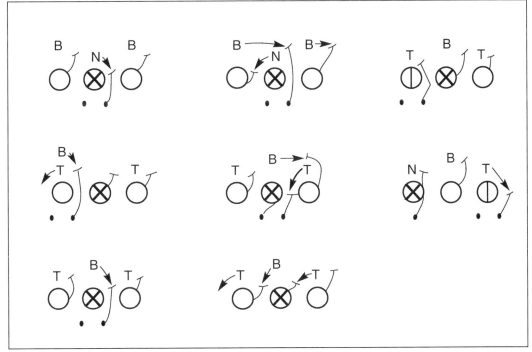

Figure 6-59. Playside zone, backside scoop

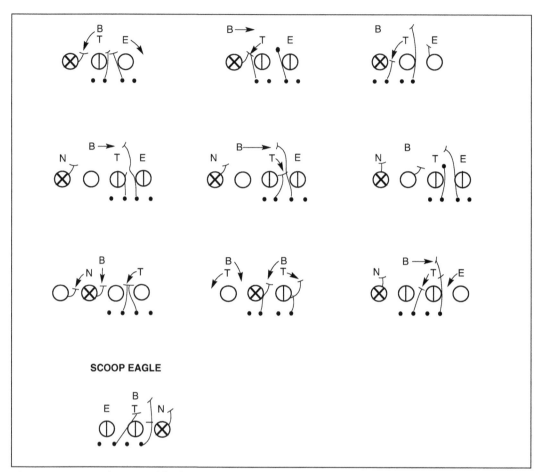

Figure 6-60. Combination blocks

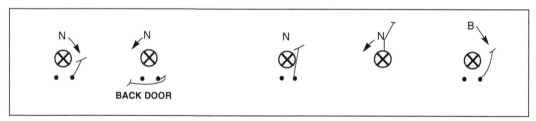

Figure 6-61. Blocking techniques for centers and guards

# Additional Defensive Numbering

The lineman in this offense knows his assignment on 95 percent of the plays. Therefore, he can concentrate on exploding off the ball and on executing the techniques required for blocking. By 95 percent, we mean blocking the 0, 1, or 2 defensive player on every play. The line will protect all gaps en route to their blocks, and all combo blocks will be automatic.

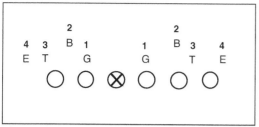

Figure 6-62. Offensive line assignments versus wide tackle 6

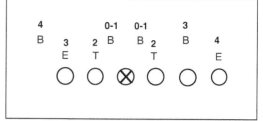

Figure 6-63. Offensive line assignments versus 4-4

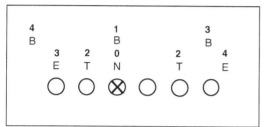

Figure 6-64. Offensive line assignments versus 5-3

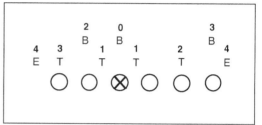

Figure 6-65. Offensive line assignments versus goal line

*Center*: Blocks 0. Snaps ball, steps hard to playside gap, and blocks man-on-man. If 0 stunts away, the center will explode on the backside 1.

*Off Guard*: Always replaces the feet of the center, thus his path will be as shown in Figure 6-67.

*On Guard*: Steps hard through the playside gap and tracks toward 1. If 2 slants, then the on guard base blocks to the outside breast of 2. This technique will lead to an automatic combo block on every play but the dive.

*On Tackle*: Explodes through outside breast of 2 (inside breast on dive play). He must not let the defender cross his face. He stays locked until he feels support from the on guard.

*Off Tackle*: Blocks 2 man through the playside gap, forcing him to the outside. Then, he takes the demolition course downfield, knocking people into a pile.

*Quarterback*: Calls the play and snap count. The center breaks and covers the ball quickly. The quarterback then calls the play again, and the rest of the team breaks the huddle on the command, "Ready, block!" This command will remind the players what they are there for.

*Linemen*: Sprint to the ball and line up in the pre-hit position with forearms on thighs. With the ball covered, the defense must be ready for a play. The quarterback will command, "Team set," and the line will drop into their four-point stances similar to an Olympic sprinter. All linemen will sprint to ball when we pass. In fact, the entire team including the quarterback will always sprint to the ball after it is thrown.

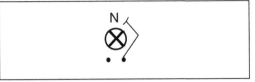

Figure 6-66. Center working playside

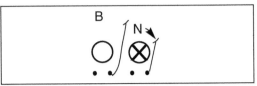

Figure 6-67. Off guard

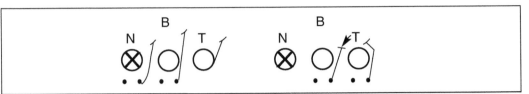

Figure 6-68. On guard

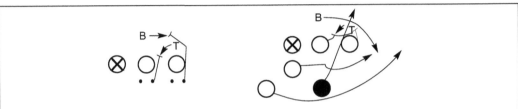

*Note*: When the dive play is called, the lineman stays locked on the double-team and lets the onside linebacker overrun the play.

Figure 6-69.

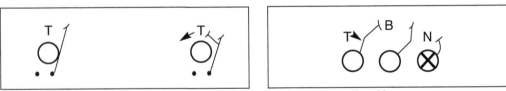

Figure 6-70. On tackle

Figure 6-71. Off tackle

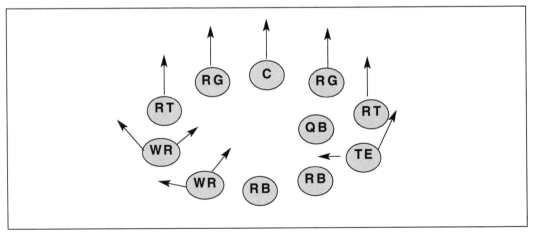

Figure 6-72. Huddle

# Attacking the Split Front

The twins formation should force the defense to take out one of the front eight and use the player to cover the inside twin. If they do not, we will attack to the splitside with a sprint-out. We will use combo routes to the flat where we have the defender outnumbered. Another strategy is to move the tight end to the splitside and put the ball in the opponent's court. Against the end over, the defense will have to radically alter their scheme. If they fail to do so, then they will be outnumbered to the strongside.

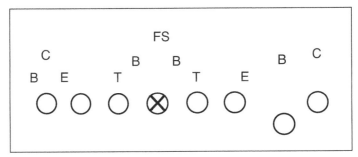

Figure 6-73. Attacking the split front

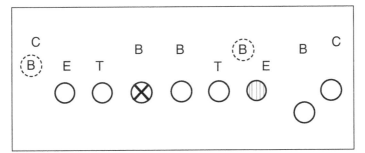

Figure 6-74. Tight end over

In the outside veer, the center is assigned to block 0. Against an odd (noseguard) defense, 0 is the noseguard. The center steps playside 45 degrees. If the noseguard steps with him, the center blocks him, keeping his head to the playside. If the noseguard comes off backside, we assign the backside guard to block him. The center should then continue downfield on his 45-degree angle, seeking to block the playside linebacker. Unless the playside linebacker is stunting inside, the center will usually end up blocking the backside linebacker along his pursuit path.

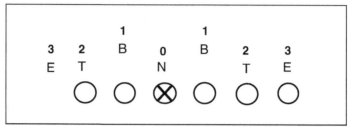

Figure 6-75. Numbering outside veer

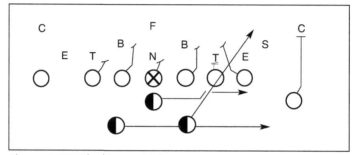

Figure 6-76. Blocking outside veer

Against an odd defense, the backside guard scoop blocks. He is taught to "replace the steps" of our center, expecting to block the noseguard. If he does not find the noseguard to the backside of our center, he will continue downfield to block the backside linebacker. The backside tackle also scoop blocks.

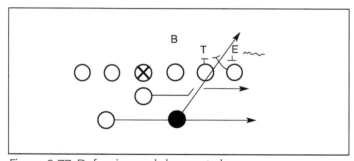

Figure 6-77. Defensive end does not close

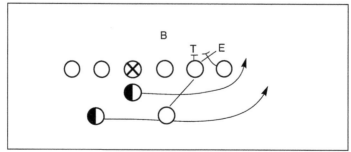

Figure 6-78. Defensive end closes

The playside guard steps playside at 45 degrees. He is assigned to block 1 (the linebacker in this case) through his playside gap. If the defensive tackle slants inside, he will block him with the help of our playside tackle. If the defensive tackle drifts outside, the offensive guard will work onto the next level and block the linebacker. The playside tackle blocks 2. He steps with his playside foot, attempting to gain outside position on the defensive tackle. He will be involved in a double-team. Depending on the movement of the defensive tackle, his partner in the double-team will be the tight end or the playside guard.

Figure 6-79. Defensive tackle fights inside/outside

# Offensive Line Drill

### Two-on-Two

*Equipment Needed*: Two footballs and three stand-up dummies
*Description*: Form two lines, one for ballcarriers and the other for defensive linemen. Establish another line of offensive blockers and set up two dummies 10 yards apart. Place two offensive blockers nose-to-nose with two defensive players inside of the two dummies. The ballcarrier is behind the offensive blockers, with a football in hand. The coach is behind the defensive player. The coach will signal the offensive blockers and the ballcarrier where to attack the defense—right, left, or middle.
*Coaching Points*:
- It should be "full go" contact.
- Let the offense win to gain confidence.
- Give praise for proper technique and effort.
- Action begins on the cadence count.

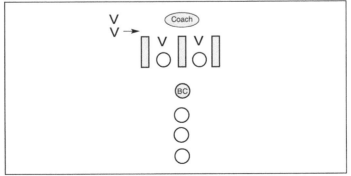

Figure 6-80. Two-on-two

## The 10 Commandments for Offensive Linemen

- Think quickly because every play is a 100-meter dash.
- Never let the opponent know that you are tired. This offense is quick tempo.
- Your first move is outward, never upward.
- Remember that every play starts with a snap and ends with a whistle.
- Never follow a missed block into your backfield.
- You have someone to block on every play. If you didn't get a block on the play, then we only had 10 men.
- Be a heavy hitter. If you're not going to use your shoulder pads, then take them off because they are slowing you down.
- Always work upfield by clearing each level as you advance.
- Get yourself a splatter block on every play.
- If you can dominate your defender, exploit the fact and don't play down to his level.

# Practicing In Hot Weather

The death from heat stroke of Minnesota Viking tackle Corey Stringer during the team's 2002 training camp forcefully reminded coaches and administrators of the dangers of heat-related illness. Following are some simple guidelines to help athletes avoid heat problems during humid practice days. Adequate water intake is the most important factor in preventing heat injury, especially among football players. Because of the protective equipment they wear and their heavy body weight, football players should consume plenty of foods such as fresh salads and fruit, which contain needed water and electrolytes. A suggested regimen for fluid intake to prevent heat illness is as follows:

- Two hours before practice, consume four (8-ounce) glasses of water.
- Fifteen minutes before practice, consume two (8-ounce) glasses of water.
- Every 15 to 30 minutes during practice, consume more water. The coaches are mindful about water breaks as I observe on occasion.
- After practice, consume five to six large glasses of cold water, as it is absorbed faster.

Many studies have shown that a well-balanced diet should provide adequate amounts of potassium and sodium needed by the athlete to prevent heat illness. Therefore, salt tablets are not beneficial. (When I played high school and college football, they insisted that we take salt tablets.) You need only increase a player's fluid intake to prevent heat illness. For every pound of weight lost, there should be an intake of one quart (4 cups) of fluid to replenish the water loss.

This generation is addicted to soda pop, which provides no help at all on the playing field. Sugar (as in soda pop) should not be included in fluids athletes drink because of (but not limited to) the following reasons:

- It delays water absorption.
- It causes fullness and sometimes nausea, which decreases the desire for fluids.
- It causes a rise in insulin levels, which will cause a subsequent decrease in blood-sugar level.

In conclusion, no magic diet will give any athlete an unfair advantage over anyone else, but a proper diet can provide the edge a player may need to compete to the best of his abilities.

Scott Ertle, Stillwater Gazette

A proper diet can provide the edge a player may need to compete to the best of his abilities.

# 7

# The Kicking Game

The spread punt is the most important play a team will participate in during the course of a ballgame. More games are won or lost because of excellence or sloppiness in the punting game than any other phase of football. You have to be great on punting downs. It must be practiced as much as your favorite offensive plays.

## Spread Punt

Any kicking play initiated by a center's snap has to be successful and must be executed with perfection in the following five stages, stemming from the offensive huddle:

- Alignment
- Snap
- Protection
- Kick
- Coverage

*Purpose*: The spread punt is used as a defensive weapon. The goal is to gain ground on every exchange of punts until you have driven the opposition deep into their territory. A punter has to have good hands; if necessary, use your quarterback. No matter how far an interior lineman can punt, it is not worth the risk of his mishandling a bad snap.

We use this type of spread punt because it allows our coverage to better release while giving the kicker proper protection. The linemen must not allow the defenders to make contact with the kicker. We tell our linemen to lock on the inside foot and block through the outside breast before releasing downfield.

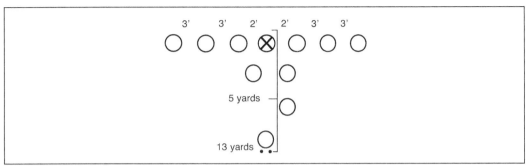

Figure 7-1. Spread punt

*Two-Point Stance*: Coverage and protection teams employ this stance with feet under armpits and with hollow in the back.

Figure 7-2. Two-point stance

## Responsibilities

*Center*: His first responsibility is always a perfect snap into the kicker's hands at all times. He should look the ball into the kicker's hands. After snapping the ball back in 0.7 seconds, he must get his head up and butt through anyone over him, and then sprint to the football.

*Guards*: They take a split of two feet. Their split should never be so great as to allow more than one man at a time to penetrate the gap. A guard keeps his inside foot in place momentarily and blocks out, and then he butts through the defensive man and sprints to cover two yards inside the hash mark.

*Tackles*: They take a split whereby they can block halfway back to the guard—generally 36 inches. A tackle must not increase this split, because he will have to block in if two men are between him and the guard. If two men are not between the tackle and the guard, the tackle keeps his inside foot in place momentarily and blocks out. He butts through the defensive man and sprints to cover three yards outside the hash mark.

*Ends*: They take a split whereby they can block all the way back to the tackle. An end must block in if two men are between the guard and tackle or if two men are between the tackle and him. Otherwise, he should keep his inside foot in place momentarily and block out, and then butt through the defensive man and sprint to cover and contain as deep as the ball has been kicked. He should never get closer than six yards from the sideline.

*Bullets*: They take a position in the gap between the guard and center at least one yard behind the ball. Normally, they should position the gap from inside and block the first rusher to break through the gap, and then butt through the defensive player and sprint to cover the kick as a linebacker (between guard and tackle). If a bullet gets no rush on his side, he should sprint to the ball, making himself as big as possible.

*Body Guard*: He takes a position five yards from behind the ball on the side of the punter, straddling the bullets' outside leg. He should block the most dangerous rusher, particularly the rusher on the punter's side. After blocking through the rusher, the body guard covers the kick as a safety. He must always block forward to the ball, and never step backward or get knocked into the kicker's path. He should supply cover directly to the ball as a secondary support. At the snap, he should look outside, inside, backside—in that order.

*Kicker*: He lines up with his kicking foot directly behind the ball at least 13 yards deep. He must look the ball into his hands, and work to get the ball into the air in 2.0 seconds from the snap. After kicking, he covers as a safety on the side of the return. The kicker must always be aware of down and distance.

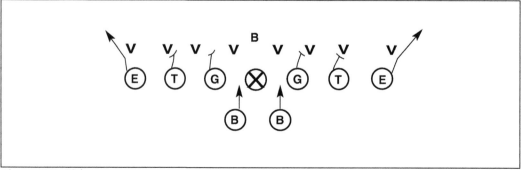

Figure 7-3. Kicker

Figure 7-4. A blocker must hit and block through the defender's outside breast before releasing to cover the kick

## Coverage

*Objectives*:

- Be there to recover safety's fumble.
- Cause fumble and recover it.
- Hold opposition to less than three yards per return.
- Break down and focus on the receiver's belt buckle.

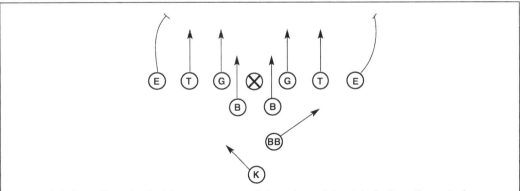

*Note*: Left bullet will run behind the receiver on a fair catch, and the right bullet will stop in front.

Figure 7-5. Coverage

Each position should carry out his protection responsibility, then sprint, gaining width and keeping his relationship to his teammates with respect to the field and the ball. Covering punts is based on running (which is nothing more than pride and desire). Each player must make his mind up that he has to sprint full speed 30 to 35 yards and be there with the ball. Kicking-team players should fan out; they must not bunch up. First man down (sprinter) throws at the safety. Even if he misses, he will force the receiver off balance and set up the coverage to tackle. If the receiver has fumbled, the tackler should drive through him and let coverage get the ball. Coverage must come under control, in a football position, never crossing their legs. They should gang tackle and get the ball. The tackles must remember that most returns are designed to split them from their ends. Keeping this fact in mind, they approach the safety from the outside. Cardinal rule: Don't be offside. Field-goal attempts must be covered just like punts. If the kicker skies the ball and the safety gives a fair-catch signal in the danger zone, the first man down should "faceguard" (i.e., protect) the goal line, and be ready to down the ball outside the goal line. We tell our players to assume a hitting position (butts down, antennas up) when breaking down in front of the ballcarrier so that they can react under control. They should not just dive by the ballcarrier or flag helplessly at him.

# Extra Point and Field Goal

Like the punt, extra point and field goal is a crucially important play in the offense. When we go in this formation, it means points for us. We use jumbos on this unit because they are hard to get around and can provide us with a solid wall.

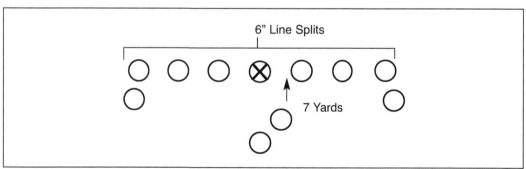

Figure 7-6. Extra point and field goal

## Responsibilities

*Center*: He makes a perfect snap any time after "ready." He should bridge up and be big after the snap.
*Linemen*: They get into a two-point stance and watch the ball. On the snap, they make a short drop step with the inside foot and slide shoulders and extended flippers to the inside. They keep the outside foot in place and get big.

*Upbacks*: They align six inches inside and six inches behind outside foot of ends. They keep their inside foot in place and block inside out.

Players must cover all field-goal attempts after they hear the ball kicked. They spread out and play the ball just as they would cover a punt. If the snap of the holder is muffed, both the kicker and holder will yell "Fire." Be alert for a no-huddle if time is a factor on a field-goal attempt.

## Fire Responsibilities

*Ends and Backs*: They release to flat areas.
*Linemen*: They reach block to the outside and stay locked on. They should not look around.

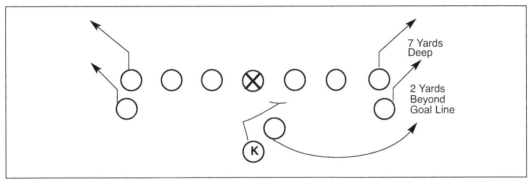

Figure 7-7. Fire

# Punt Return

## Responsibilities

The following duties are for return right. They should be mirrored for return left.

*Safety*: He forces the punt and attempts to block it. Then, he gets to the return and escorts ballcarrier to the end zone.
*Ends*: They drive hard into their man, watch the punt leave, and then sprint to set up a wall. The end on the return side may have an aggressive crash block.
*Tackles*: They drive hard into their man, watch the punt, and then sprint to form the wall. They maintain a three- to six-yard spacing and turns clockwise to the inside.
*Noseguard*: He drives hard into the center and the bullet on the side of the return, sprints to the wall, and turns clockwise to the inside.
*Right Linebacker*: He checks for a fake, hovers in inside, and screen blocks the first man up the middle away from the return.
*Left Linebacker*: He checks for fake, sprints to crash-block the outside force on the reverse side.

*Upback*: He fair catches a short punt; on a deep punt, he blocks the most dangerous tackler.

*Deep Back*: He reads blocks, shoots through a seam to the wall, and sprints to the goal line.

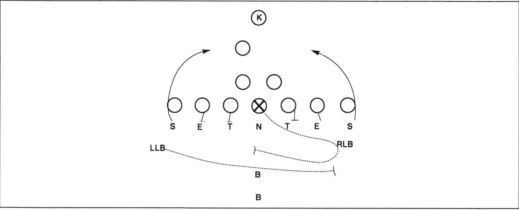

Figure 7-8. Punt return

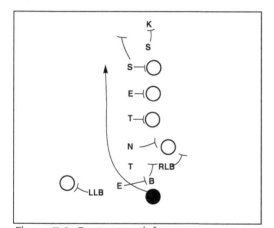

Figure 7-9. Punt return left

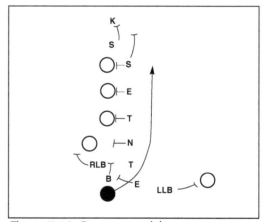

Figure 7-10. Punt return right

# Kickoff Return

### Front Wall

*1*: He sprints down/across field to the 20; he is responsible for first man outside of hash and/or wall.

*2-5*: They sprint back 15 yards, bump attackers, and then sprint downfield three yards outside of the hash and form a wall. They turn to the inside with a clockwise turn.

*Wedge*: He uses the wedge middle technique. The safety on the return side must peel to the outside to pick up the first man down inside of the wall. If no attacker is dangerous at that point, the safety should lead back up to the goal line. The wedge must make the return appear to be a return middle.

## Backs

*Blocker*: He follows the wedge middle until last possible instant. He veers outside to the wall and blocks the first dangerous attacker.

*Ballcarrier*: He follows wedge middle until last possible instant. He veers to the wall and sprints to the goal line.

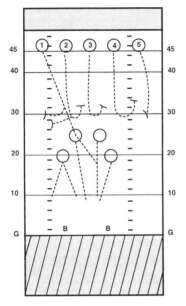

Figure 7-11. Fake wedge wall right (left)— position no. 1

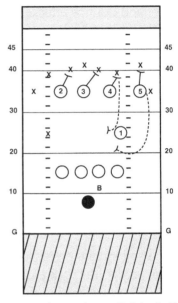

Figure 7-12. Fake wedge wall right (left)— position no. 2

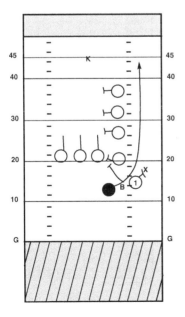

Figure 7-13. Fake wedge wall right (left)— position no. 3

# Wedge Middle

### Front Wall

*3:* He sprints back to the 30-yard line and picks up first attacker in middle third of the field.

*2 and 4:* They sprint back to the 26- to 29-yard line. They pinch to the inside, wall off the middle, and bounce attackers to the outside.

*1 and 5:* They sprint back between the 30- and 33-yard line inside of the hash. They bounce attackers to outside.

### Wedge

*Point Men:* They sprint back to the ball. They keep a 7- to 10-yard cushion, sprint upfield shoulder-to-shoulder through the chute, and run a 100-yard dash to the goal line.

*Wing Men:* They sprint back to the ball. They keep a 7- to 10-yard cushion, run shoulder-to-shoulder with the point men, and sprint to the goal line. An outside safety may peel off the wedge to block an outside attacker threatening the ballcarrier.

### Backs

*Blocker:* He sprints to the wedge and takes up the safety position on his side. He may peel off the wedge to block an outside attacker threatening the ballcarrier.

*Ballcarrier:* He sprints behind the wedge, looks for a seam at the point of contact with attackers, and sprints to the goal line.

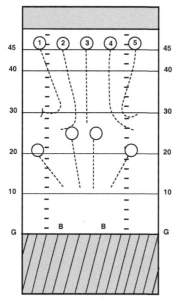

Figure 7-14. Wedge middle—position no. 1

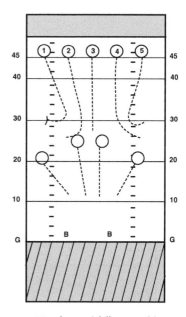

Figure 7-15. Wedge middle—position no. 2

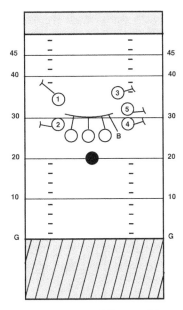

Figure 7-16. Wedge middle—position no. 3

# Punt Block

This play will be used right before the half or the end of the game when something needs to happen.

### Rush Side

*Linebacker*: He aligns outside the widest man, gets off on the snap of the ball, and blocks the kick.
*Cornerback*: He aligns inside shoulder of the widest man, gets off on the ball through inside gap, and blocks the kick.
*End*: He aligns head-up with the second man from outside, drives straight through the opponent's outside eye, and does not let him reach center.
*Tackle*: He aligns head-up with the third man from outside, gets off on the ball, and drives through the opponent's outside eye demanding his block.
*Noseguard*: He aligns head-up with the center, gets off on the ball, slips to the side of the ball, and blocks the kick.

### Away Side

*Tackle*: He aligns head-up with the third man from the outside. He gets off on the ball and demands the block of the upback. When the ball is kicked, he peels for return to his side.
*End*: He aligns head-up with second man from the outside, drives through him, and blocks the kick. If the ball gets kicked, he peels and sets the wall.

*Cornerback*: He aligns head-up with the widest man. He comes out early and covers the outside receiver. When the ball is kicked, the cornerback blocks the first man inside.
*Linebacker*: He aligns outside the widest man, gets off on the ball, and blocks the kick.
*Safety*: He covers the receiver on the side of the block, communicates with the returner, and blocks the first dangerous man.
*Returner*: He fields the ball and gets upfield to the wall.

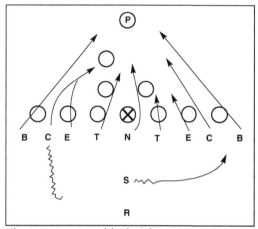

Figure 7-17. Punt block right

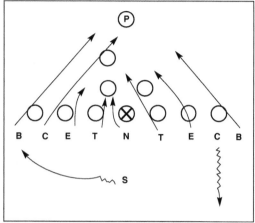

Figure 7-18. Punt block left

# Extra-Point and Field-Goal Block

## Responsibilities

*Noseguard*: He aligns head-up on the center and charges hard.
*Tackles*: They align head-up on the guard on their side and charge hard.
*Ends*: They align head-up on the end blockers, drive into them, and shed to the outside lane for containment.
*Corners*: They align outside the tight ends, rush the kick, and lay out in front of the ball.
*Linebackers*: They align head-up on 2 and cover him man-to-man.
*Strong Safety*: He aligns outside the back on the right side and covers him man-to-man.
*Weak Safety*: He aligns outside the back on the left side and covers him man-to-man.

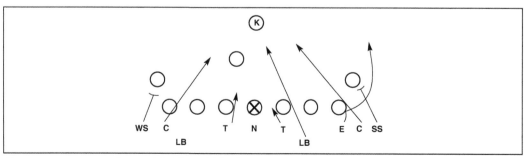

Figure 7-19. Extra-point and field-goal block

# Kickoff Coverage

Kickoff coverage requires a bunch of hard-nosed types who want to run downfield, square up, and hit something. They want to tackle the ballcarrier inside the 20-yard line and run off the field with high fives. We like to use linebackers and defensive backs because they're generally better at changing direction and remaining under control. This unit sets the tempo at the start of the game or the half. This unit is not a place to allow your timid souls to experience high school football.

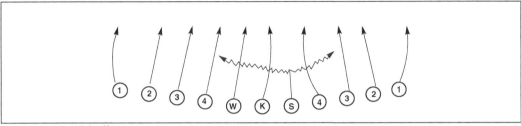

Figure 7-20. Kickoff coverage

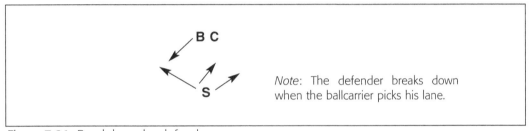

*Note*: The defender breaks down when the ballcarrier picks his lane.

Figure 7-21. Breakdown by defender

## Responsibilities

*Kicker*: He runs down and breaks the wedge unless he is slightly built or can run fast. If the kicker has wheels, then he can play safety on the kickoff.

*Safety*: This position requires speed. The safety releases downfield and avoids contact. He floats to the ballcarrier, allows a 10-yard cushion, and takes the field away. This technique can be mastered quickly.

*1s*: Ends or outside contain types run downfield at six yards from sideline. He should not allow the ballcarrier to get outside of him, and turn everything back into the inside.

*2s*: Defensive back or contain types move downfield and avoid everyone until they get 20 yards from the ball; then, they pursue hard in their lanes.

*3s*: Linebacker types explode downfield in his lane. He should avoid being blocked and be prepared to attack the blocker and charge the ballcarrier.

*4s*: Linebacker or quick linemen types should think of themselves as wedge breakers and attack in their lanes.

# Onside Kick Coverage

We will use the onside kick as a surprise play or as a last-ditch effort to win a game that is getting away from us. With a ratio of 4:1 failure, the odds are not good enough for us. We are not great believers that the onside is good strategy against a superior opponent. If it fails or if you don't score as a result of your efforts, it can backfire against you. We prefer its use versus a weaker opponent. Since we use our quickest players on the regular coverage team, few player changes are needed except the placement of your very best on the playside.

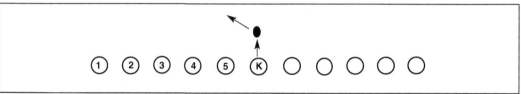

Figure 7-22. Onside kick

Place your five toughest and fastest stud ducks on the playside. Players 2 and 4 block the first two defenders from outside in. Players 1, 3, and 5 sprint all out to the football.

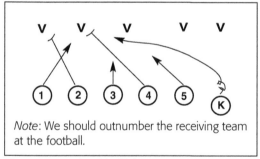

*Note*: We should outnumber the receiving team at the football.

Figure 7-23. Onside kick coverage

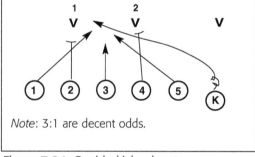

*Note*: 3:1 are decent odds.

Figure 7-24. Onside kick advantage

Never have your team kick the ball out of bounds. Be aware that sometimes the defense sends too many players near the forward line, and signal that you want to kick it deeper.

# Onside Kick Receiving

We always teach our players to expect an onside kick every time out. On those occasions where we are certain that this is the case, we insert our hands team. The hands team consists of players with good hands like running backs, quarterbacks, defensive backs and tight ends. Centers, guards, and tackles need not apply for obvious reasons. We ask that players be smart, tough, and quick.

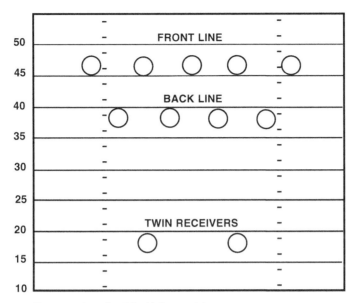

Figure 7-25. Onside kick receiving

## Rules for the Hands Team

- Do not attempt to pick up the ball and return it. This situation is high-risk.
- Judge the speed of the ball, because it may be better to let it go out of bounds rather than handle it.
- Look to block if the ball is kicked deep.
- Some teams will try a line drive kick in hopes that the ball will be fumbled. Let the ball pass you unless you are certain you can cover the ball.
- Fall on the ball and cradle it under your body and wrap with the legs.

# Appendix A:
# Third-and-Long

**Jerry Foley**

How many times have you heard from coaches and parents alike that this group or team has great potential? *Webster's Dictionary* defines potential as "something that can develop, or may become actual: existing in possibility only." Potential by itself can be a meaningless attribute because of all the "ifs" involved. Like any other trait, potential must be groomed and nurtured to bring it to full bloom. The successful coach is able to motivate his players to rise to the occasion and to be the springboard that enables them to fully realize their potential.

Motivational methods and techniques are diversified and come in a variety of packages. The successful coach, CEO, boss, or administrator is able to reach his charges, stimulating them to perform at peak efficiency and beyond—not always an easy task. What motivates one individual may have just the opposite effect upon the guy standing next to him. The adept motivator will possess a plethora of techniques to aid him in pushing the starter buttons of all involved. Productive coaches and teachers are not only leaders, but great motivators as well.

Having worked side-by-side and shoulder-to-shoulder with George Thole for the past three decades, I have witnessed firsthand a coach who is continuously able to get his players to perform well beyond the conscious level. The kids in the program always come first. In the event of a loss, blame is not directed at the players. Responsibility for the loss is shouldered by the coaching staff. He tells them that they were outplayed, and we were out coached.

Although an excellent tactician and leader and extremely knowledgeable about the game of football, I believe George to be the consummate motivator. You do not establish a record of 285 wins, 69 losses, and 2 ties, while averaging 9.23 victories per season over a 32-year career as a head coach because you have a corral full of great athletes ever year. To have great athletes every year is utopian of course, and the dream of every coach. George teaches a college-level course for graduate credit on methods and means of how to motivate and maximize a performer's achievement level. The class is well attended by high school and college educators, administrators, counselors, and coaches.

Motivation has a lot to do with developing a sound attitude amongst your players. An oft-repeated slogan heard on our campus is, "You don't have to be a great athlete to play football at Stillwater High School, but you must have a great attitude." We can all agree that every participant is capable of developing a sound, positive learning attitude.

While most successful high school football programs may have two or three "blue chip" type players available to them, they must fill out their rosters with average and sometimes below-average athletes. Unless you are able to recruit your players, you must play the hand you are dealt. The onus of winning or losing then lies with the coaching staff's ability to motivate and blend this mixture into a viable group capable of competing successfully week in and week out.

In actuality, X's and O's play but a miniscule roll in determining the success or failure of any football program, particularly at the high school level. Leadership, discipline, teamwork, intensity, integrity, courage, and hard work by players and staff, combined with generous amounts of motivation, are the ingredients that spell success.

Besides being able to motivate players and staff by his very presence, George institutes a variety of motivational happenings to further motivate and inspire those associated with him. He sets high standards and lofty goals for those around him and does not accept mediocrity from anyone—himself, his staff, or his players.

## A Matter of Urgency

Sideline organization is a high-priority item during a football game for the Stillwater High School Ponies. Whether at home or on the road, precise procedures are carried out to the letter. While the defensive types align to the right of the 50-yard marker along with the defensive coordinator, the offensive players stay to the left of the 50 with their respective coaches. Assistant coaches patrol the sideline making certain players stay well behind the chalk line separating them from the boundary markers. Three-deep depth charts dictate the alignment of the players along the sideline as to their immediacy in the total game plan. Players are schooled to be attentive and alert with their minds as to what was happening on the field at all times. Special-teams players, in a state of readiness, stay close to their position coaches throughout the entire game. It is their responsibility to react and be on the field with their special team. Failure to do so results in their removal from that specialty team until further notice. "If you snooze, you lose."

With a change of possession, the players coming off the field report immediately to their position coaches to deal with any adjustments that had to be made. After critiquing the players, they are dismissed to get a drink of water, make an equipment adjustment, or just relax and get off of their feet. These sideline procedures allow the coaching staff to know exactly where key players are located at all times during the game, thus negating the necessity to holler up and down the sideline looking for a particular player.

The organization on the field makes it possible for the head coach to move freely up and down the sideline, giving him access to the whole squad and the entire coaching staff. This organization frees him up, allowing immediate input on all aspects of the game.

By his very nature, Thole is a presence on the sideline during a Pony football game. He is active and very much into all phases of the game. Although in control, being confined by wearing headphones is not his forte. He is animated and is sometimes an "in-your-face" type of mentor. He likes being available and to be able to move to where the action was, thus allowing him to make needed adjustments and corrections.

Through the years, on more that one occasion, George has been seen hurrying up the sideline to talk to a player or a staff member. Sometimes, people would ask what George and I were arguing about during the course of the game. I would respond that I didn't recall us having an argument at any point during the contest. They countered by stating that they had seen him run up to me, gesticulating and getting in my face in what appeared to be an all-out disagreement between us. In actuality, many emotional encounters occur between coaches during the heat of battle. With the competitive juices flowing, combined with the adrenalin rush that accompanies competition, looks can be and often are misleading to the outsider. In the heat of the moment, what appears to be an all-out confrontation merely amounts to a rapid interchange of ideas between highly motivated individuals, brought on by a sudden change in the game plan.

When George speaks, he wants total eye contact and your complete attention. With his face a mere three inches from yours, it is difficult not to possess both. In reality, what he has to say has nothing to do with his being mad or upset. It has to do with getting the message across posthaste. An unforeseen or sudden mishap at a crucial moment of the game triggers such a response. Getting his thoughts across as soon as possible to players and staff alike is, in Thole-speak, simply "a matter of urgency."

## Thole and the Jumbos

It is a given that the head coach assumes responsibility for the success or the failure of his program, and as such, must be thoroughly schooled in all phases of the sport. In high school football programs around the state, although responsible for all aspects of the game, the majority of head coaches seem to ally themselves on the offensive side of the ball. At Stillwater Area High School, while George shoulders all of the burdens that accompany the title of head coach, he is at his best when coaching the offensive linemen.

Offensive linemen, by their very nature, are a different group of individuals, often being the quiet, unassuming types—some so quiet that you are scarcely aware of their presence on the practice field. Through the years, these individuals have a tendency to matriculate toward the offensive line along with their peers because they may lack the speed or the finesse required of the so-called skilled positions. However, these are the same guys we ask to play down in the dirt where the game is really played with little chance of recognition or fan appreciation for their efforts. Offensive linemen are not going to be in the headlines following a big victory. Their reward is the simple realization that they gave their team the opportunities it needed to win the game. It takes a special type of coach, working continuously in season and out, to nurture these young aspirants to bring them to their full potential.

Being a former lineman himself, George has a way of getting into their psyche, establishing among them a strong feeling of pride and self-worth. Along with being a taskmaster insisting on all out hustle and enthusiasm, he is a stickler for proper technique and execution by all of his linemen. Daily work in the chutes, under his discriminate eye, ensures progress in the quickness and footwork necessary in getting off the ball, both individually and as a unit.

Thole is a master of technique when it comes to training down linemen. More important, I believe, is his ability to get the maximum out of players who by design are not naturally aggressive types. He is able to get in their face, lighting a fire in them, and at the same time, he can transmit his inner feelings toward them. George can chew a kid up and down one minute and in the next minute have him walking on air. They come to understand that he respects not only who they are, but their importance to our program.

Arguably, one of the more difficult positions to coach year in and year out, Stillwater has come up with offensive lines that have enabled the Pony offense to dominate their opponents, averaging 30 plus points per game over a 26-year span. George takes young men of average playing ability and molds them into a cohesive unit that performs with confidence and self-assuredness. He has empathy for every member of the team, but the "jumbos" are special. They truly play for the love of the game.

## Stars, Skulls, and Splatters

Many college and high school football programs award their players with helmet decals for making big plays against the previous week's opponent. These stickers are varied and often coincide with the team's nickname or logo. Whatever the decal, players display them on their helmets with great pride and a sense of accomplishment, not unlike the gunslinger of the old West with notches on his gun belt. The awards are given out for a variety of feats that occur throughout the course of a football game. They may be awarded for touchdowns, touchdown blocks, fumble recoveries, solo tackles, blocked punts, and such. Because many of these are individual awards, coaches must exercise caution so as not to lose sight of the all-important team concept. As the old saying points out, there is no "I" in the word "team."

At Stillwater High School, to emphasize the concept that the team comes first, awards are given out only when the team was victorious. In a losing effort, no awards are made even though some players may have had a career-type game. When the team plays well and attains victory, everyone participates in the awards celebration. Our system is unique in some ways, and at the same time, similar to other team-award programs. Our players take pride in the fact that awards are made only in victory and not in defeat.

Stars are offensive awards and were given for the usual offensive accomplishments such as touchdowns, touchdown blocks, domination blocks, touchdown passes, controlling the line of scrimmage, and so on, while skulls are defensive awards and given for solo tackles, interceptions, fumble recoveries, blocked punts, sacks, and the like. The splatter decal is a special award given for the big hit, either offensively or defensively. The splatter is coveted because by connotation it identifies the recipient as a big hitter in a hitter's game.

Helmet decals are also given to entire teams for their consistent play. For example, if the kickoff team holds the opponents' returns inside the 20-yard line throughout the entire game, each member of the kickoff team is recognized. Likewise, extra-point teams are rewarded after a multiple of successful attempts as are punt-coverage teams for consistency in their coverage. Kickers and punters are also identified for things like end-zone kicks and pinpoint punting. All in all, almost every member of the team has the opportunity to win an award on game night if the team won the game.

Our awards are given out Saturday mornings following the successful outcome of Friday night's game. A big "to-do" is a major part of the ceremonies, which are light-hearted and full of pizzazz. The players savor the moment as they had the opportunity to see and to interact with their coaches in a relaxed and unstructured setting. The players are actively involved in the festivities and the price of being a first-time award recipient is to entertain the rest of the team with a song, a poem, a dance, or some other bit of folderol.

# The Great Tholenac: Whatever it Takes

Years ago on late night television, Johnny Carson was the star of the popular *Tonight Show.* To keep audiences tuned in and ratings up, Carson developed a variety of skits starring himself in the role of any number of humorous aliases. One of his better-known characters was the "Great Carnac," a mysterious soothsayer possessing mystic powers. Johnny came on stage dressed in a floor length robe and cape with a huge turban on his head. His straight man, Ed McMahon, after giving an elaborate introduction, would hand him sealed envelopes, which the Great One would meditate on and conjure up the answer to the question contained within. The audience loved it.

In the ongoing effort to add more vitality to our awards ceremony following a victory, George came up with the idea that someone other than one of the coaches should be invited to present the decals and awards to the recipients—hence, the "Great Tholenac" was born. Playing the straight man, I would announce to the team the immanent arrival of "the all-seeing, the all-knowing, that great purveyor of messages from beyond, a soothsayer without rival, the one, the only, the Great Tholenac." Tholenac appeared in full costume greeted by the enthusiastic applause of his captive audience. After bowing and other mystic formalities, he would demand total silence so as to not interfere with his karma. I would then explain that I had in my possession three envelopes that had been hermetically sealed in a mayonnaise jar and locked safely away in the vault in the local courthouse. The contents of each envelope contained a secret question unknown to all present. Tholenac's task was to be able, through his mystic powers, to answer the question before the seal on the envelope was broken. With great concentration and with eyes closed, he would hold the sealed envelope to his brow while meditating deeply. (Sometimes, the presence of disbelievers would play havoc with his vibes.) Occasionally, Tholenac dozed off whilst his expectant audience awaited his response.

While holding the envelope to his forehead and mustering up total concentration so as to be in touch with the netherworld, Tholenac would slowly intone the answer to the unknown question in the sealed envelope. For example, Tholenac would say, "Zip-a-dee-doo-dah," and repeat, "Zip-a-dee-doo-dah is the answer." He would then ceremoniously open the envelope and read the question inside. In this case, the question was, "What do you do when your doo-dah is open?" A similar Tholenac comes to mind, the answer being, "Yucca dew." The question was, "What do you find on your yucca in the morning?" Another favorite, "Buccaneer is the answer." The question was, "What is one hell of a price to pay for corn?" He would do three or four of these "Tholenacs," then proceed to hand out the game awards.

People in the Valley were constantly giving George or someone on the staff a call informing them of a new "Tholenac" they had just heard. Through the years, he developed and kept a complete file of them, numbering in the hundreds. Tholenac first appeared on the scene in the early 1970s and was present at each and every Pony football victory over a span of 20-plus years. (He was a frontrunner and never showed up after a loss.) He disappeared sometime in the mid 1990s. One fall, George informed the team that he had received an urgent telegram stating that Tholenac was last seen floating in a life raft somewhere in the south Pacific. He has not been seen or heard from since.

## Gentlemen, Start Your Engines

One year, George and a few of the local fans had the opportunity to attend the Indy 500 at the Indianapolis Speedway. Impressed by the aura surrounding this sporting spectacular, Thole returned home with a souvenir replica of the famous checkered flag used when starting the race. Just prior to our players leaving the locker room for the opening kickoff and at the close of the pre-game talk, he would wave the flag vigorously and shout, "Gentlemen, start your engines!" With their competitive juices flowing and eager to get it on, the players stormed out of the locker room and onto the field ready to play. Throughout the season, the flag held a prominent place on the sideline, and it wasn't long before checkered flags began to appear in the stands. By the season's end, the home stands were filled with cheering fans waving their checkered flags.

## Ward Cleaver Night

Many readers will remember Ward Cleaver, the compassionate, all-American father characterized in the popular sitcom *Leave It To Beaver* of the late 1950s and early1960s. Ward never became upset or frustrated. He had a calm, serene way of handling any and all situations, good or bad, while guiding and directing such situations into results that were comforting and satisfying to all involved. Utilization of this type of behavior gave birth on game nights to what we refer to as "Ward Cleaver Nights." Such a night meant that everything was going smoothly for our team both offensively and defensively. George could leisurely roam the sidelines relaxed and content because of the absence of any problems occurring from the game field. Because things were going so well, his major concern was to be able to "make the run." Making the run meant that we were able to get every player in uniform into the football game that night. A Ward Cleaver night also meant that the head coach never had to get upset or raise his voice, but that he could just be relaxed and laid back and casually ask, "Gee, Wally, has everyone gotten into the game yet?" Needless to say, the players reveled when, because of their hard work at practice during the week, game nights turned into Ward Cleaver nights.

# Or Maybe You Want to Go to a Movie

An additional motivational ploy in our program also began sometime in the early 1970s. Steve Forseth, who coached linebackers and defensive ends, as well as serving as the Ponies' strength coach, teamed up with George as would-be movie critics (Siskel and Ebert they were not). Upon completion of practice the evening before the game, Coach Thole would gather the entire squad together to review the itinerary to be followed over the next 24-hour period prior to game time. He reminded them of the normal procedures to be followed on the night before a football game: "Stay away from junk food. Get plenty of rest. Watch a sporting event on TV. Abide by the curfew—or maybe you want to go to a movie."

George and Steve, feeding off each other, would then expound on what movies were playing at Mall One and Mall Two in beautiful downtown Stillwater. The movie titles, mostly fictitious, were woven into some kind of warped plot, but the casts were always real. They included such notables as Randolph Scott, Tom Mix, Marlene Dietrich, Bette Davis, and Mickey Rooney, to name a few, while the big star of every movie was Rex, the Wonder Horse. It was a good way to end the week's practice and wind down while getting into a proper frame of mind for the following night's game. Soon, the event became tradition, and the players were quick to ask, "Coach, what's playing at the movies tonight?"

# Geno and Taco-isms

Gene Bealka, the athletic trainer at Stillwater High School over a span of three decades, was a mainstay of the sideline of every Pony football game. Besides tending to the sick and wounded, "Taco," as he was affectionately called, was somewhat of a big brother and father figure to the athletes. Players not only admired and respected him, but were able to confide in him as well. Along with his adeptness at treating and preventing injuries and getting injured players healed and back into action as soon as possible, Geno was a bit of a philosopher. Thole, recognizing his impact on the team, had him make a regular appearance at the pre-game preparations held the evening before the game. When finished with his instructions on diet, bed rest, water intake, and sideline procedures, Taco always finished up with some words of wisdom for the team. These messages, eventually called "Taco-isms," became a ritual that players always looked forward to. An example of one of his pearls to live by was, "Some people see giants as too big to hit, while others see them as too big to miss." The pre-game routine was never complete without a Taco-ism.

# Local Support

The St. Croix Valley is fortunate to have local newspapers that give ample coverage to all Stillwater High School activities, including academic and music programs along with extra-curricular events. The *Gazette* is a daily that runs Monday through Friday, while the *Courier* and *Valley Press* are weekly publications. Football coverage includes game summaries accompanied by action photos and interviews with players and coaches. Pre-game reports list starting lineups for both the Ponies and their next opponent along with their respective win-loss records. Pony football calendars featuring the schedule along with numerous action photographs of the players, are prominently and proudly displayed in most local businesses and restaurants. Valley fans love their football and the Ponies, and local support runs high.

# Building a Coaching Staff

The following sections describe some of the thoughts and observations that I have developed over a span of three-plus decades in my role as an educator and as the offensive coordinator under head coach George Thole. They are not intended to be all-encompassing, but reflect my feelings on being a part of one of the more successful high school football coaching staffs in the state of Minnesota.

## Chain of Command

In any endeavor, whether it is in the military, the business arena, politics, or in the field of education and the world of athletics, a strong chain of command is paramount to success. Leadership is the backbone of the infrastructure and framework of any organization and is fundamental in achieving and obtaining any and all lofty goals. Lacking a steadfast hierarchy is certain to produce substandard performances and ultimately result in failure. Leadership must originate at the top of the organizational pyramid and be firmly entrenched at every level of the supervisory structure to ensure that everyone involved is aware of his responsibilities.

Great leaders are also good at delegating and surrounding themselves with competent people who are both loyal and capable of carrying out the major objectives of the organization. The skillful leader is able to identify the strong traits of his coworkers and thus place them in position to best serve and fulfill the overall objectives of the entire group. The age-old adage referring to the chain being only as strong as its weakest link is true.

## The Buck Stops Here

When hearing the terms boss, head honcho, CEO, or the "super," a singular connotation comes to the forefront, signifying someone who is totally in charge of and responsible for all of the events and happenings that occur within a given organization. For the reader who is old enough, or who is a history buff, you will recall that Harry S. Truman was the President of the United States during that critical period of American history at the close of World War II. "Give 'em hell Harry," as he was affectionately called, had a permanent placard on his desk in the oval office stating emphatically, "The buck stops here!" Although he had input and advice from his aides and staff, ultimately, the final decision to end the war fell upon his shoulders alone. Leaders are in place to lead and to make decisions that are often difficult and many times unpopular, but they must be made.

On any coaching staff, the head coach is the CEO, and final decisions and choices are ultimately his to make. Building a football staff is a unique situation in the coaching profession, if for no other reason than the sheer number of coaches involved in making up a given staff. Most high school football programs, particularly in the "metro areas" where enrollments are larger, will have anywhere from 18 to 25 or more coaches on their staffs, covering grades 9 through 12. Add to that number a dozen or more coaches at the junior high and middle school levels, and you are dealing with an overall staff of 35 to 40 coaches. Obviously, with a staff of this proportion, much more needs to be dealt with than mere X's and O's. Personalities, knowledge of the game, strengths and weaknesses of assistants, and abilities to relate with kids at varying age levels enter into the picture when shaping a viable coaching staff. Just as it is important to get players situated in positions where they are able to reach their optimum potential and best help the team, the head coach is charged with aligning his staff to maximize the opportunities for success at all levels of the total program.

When George Thole came to Stillwater High School as the head coach in the fall of 1971, football staffs were considerably smaller than they are today. Although managing the smaller staff proved to be less problematic, coaching changes still had to be made to ensure that the kids in the St. Croix Valley would have the opportunity to receive the most competent coaching possible. Through ensuing years as enrollments increased, so too did the total number of coaches involved in the program. Evidence of George's managerial skills and his ability to deal with a variety of personalities include the fact that the bulk of our high school coaching staff, with one or two exceptions, stayed intact for the full 29 years of his tenure at Stillwater Area High School. Longevity and cohesiveness of a staff forges a common bond of togetherness and resolve that aids in creating an atmosphere of success.

## Rounding Out the Staff

Whereas in college and in the pro ranks, the coach has full authority to hand pick his entire staff. The head coach at the high school level enjoys no such luxury. In contrast, he must build and mold his staff from available faculty personnel. The key then lies with his ability to assemble and coordinate a workable taskforce from within that is capable of carrying out a long-term game plan. By focusing on the strengths of the assistants available to him, he is then able to place them in a position where they can best benefit the overall program. It is helpful if the head coach is open-minded and somewhat of a psychologist so he can deal successfully with a plethora of egos and personalities. It is of primary importance that he "sells" the staff on his methods, beliefs, and doctrines along with his overall long- and short-term goals. To assure that everyone on the staff is working toward the same end, it is imperative for him to attain the unflagging loyalty of all of his aides. Without complete loyalty, his total program can become chaotic and undermined.

Ideally, varsity, junior varsity, and sophomore staffs will be manned and operated by certified and licensed teachers working within the school district. The successful staff will have a generous mix of personalities, including creative individuals who are able to "think on their feet." The career coach, one who is dedicated and signed up for the long haul, is invaluable to the program and to the head coach.

## Coffee, Napkins, and Cigars

Meetings of any kind, including football staff meetings, can be tedious, boring, and a turn-off for at least some of the people involved. Conducting a meeting for meeting's sake is generally counterproductive, and hence avoided by the resourceful leader. By their very nature, meetings have a tendency to be quite formal and sometimes seem to go on forever, stifling many of the rank-and-file participants. A productive meeting is one that begins on time and ends on time while addressing a workable agenda. Effective meetings, those that result in positive actions, are to the point and involve generous amounts of give-and-take from its participants. To be productive, the staff meeting needn't be formal or stuffy. It can be relaxed, unstructured, and an enjoyable experience for all.

Under the guidance and leadership of Coach Thole, our staff met with regularity during the active season. The off-season was exactly that, the off-season, and we concerned ourselves with other matters. The beauty of coaching football at the high school level is that it is a seasonal game and does not require year-round involvement of the entire staff. It is true, however, that the head coach's duties keep him busy throughout the entire year with behind-the-scene activities, including weight-room supervision, keeping tabs on the players' academic progress, and their general behavior as citizens in the school population. The responsibilities of the head coach are continuous and never ending. Commonly, many of the assistants on the staff are involved in coaching winter and spring sports, which consumes much of their time.

Many of our most productive staff meetings, particularly in the early years, were of a very informal nature over coffee at a local neighborhood restaurant. During two-a-day practices, we gathered at Joseph's Family Restaurant for lunch and to talk football. Besides discussing the morning's practice session, strengths, weaknesses, and personnel, among other things, we were able to firm up our game plan for the afternoon practice. These were always beneficial sessions filled with an abundance of give-and-take that produced a vast interchange of ideas and suggestions. Placement of personnel was discussed, such as which players might be two-way performers, who were the hitters on the team, which players would best fill out our special teams, what our three-deep roster would look like, along with the overall make-up and chemistry of the squad.

Following the afternoon practice, we again assembled at Joseph's for coffee or a soda to relax, enjoy an occasional cigar, and talk over the day's activities. Often, napkins substituted for clipboards as we parried and countered between offensive and defensive moves. As unstructured as these gatherings were, many of the subtleties and nuances of our offense were refined and honed there.

Once school began and the players were back in class, we shifted to our regular routine, and the gatherings at Joseph's were reduced to about once a week. These were primarily relaxing bull sessions where we could kick back, recap recent progress, and just enjoy the camaraderie. Over and above being a close-knit staff, we were all good friends.

Throughout the regular season, our staff met in the film room Saturday mornings to break down film and go over the scouting report for our next opponent. Sunday evenings, we gathered separately, offensive and defensive staffs, to finalize our game plan for the week. George made every effort to keep these Sunday night meetings from an hour and a half to a maximum of two hours. Some of our most productive meetings were of the "in-your-face" type of meeting. Fortunately, our staff was made up of strongly opinionated coaches who were not hesitant to express themselves and to make their feelings known. The last thing a head coach needs is a collection of "yes men" incapable of an original thought. Strong personalities, under the guidance of a good leader, generally evolve into a strong, productive staff. All said and done, when the ideas, suggestions and offerings were all on the table, the final say and decisions are the responsibility of the head coach. The buck does stop there.

## Maintaining the Staff

At the high school and junior high level, other than the head coach, assistants have a tendency to come and go and may be as unpredictable as the weather. Other than assembling a viable staff and placing them in suitable coaching positions, a key factor for the head coach lies in his ability to keep them in his program over the long haul. Ensuring continuity of the staff can prove to be an immeasurable asset to the program.

I can state without equivocation, that the football coaching staff at Stillwater dating from 1971 through 1999, was party to the most successful high school football program in the state of Minnesota over the longest span of time. As referred to elsewhere in this book, the vast majority of our staff, with a few exceptions, remained together for a span of 29 years. Being together season after season afforded us a continuity of program not enjoyed by many staffs. Our coaches knew from year to year exactly what their duties and responsibilities would be and were readily equipped to carry them out. As a staff, we attended numerous football clinics, keeping informed on the nuances and subtle changes in the game. Generally, when you saw one Stillwater coach at a football event, you saw 8 to 12 of us.

Questions arise like, "How does a head coach keep his assistants in his program over a long period of time? What drives a coach to continue in the role of an assistant throughout his career?" In addressing answers to questions such as these, I look inward and respond with my personal thoughts and reactions.

For 39 years, I have coached football at the high school level, the last 29 years as the offensive coordinator for George at Stillwater Area High School. Friends and associates, even members of my own family, often wondered if I had aspirations of becoming a head football coach. Upon graduation from college, I was certain that being a head coach was in my future. When hired as an assistant in 1961, I was eager to be a part of the coaching fraternity and to develop and learn the ins and outs of the profession.

Because I was the head hockey coach, along with being a varsity assistant in the football program in 1971, I was not a candidate for the head football coaching position when it became available. The athletic director at the time, C.J. Knoche, hired George away from the powerful Richfield High School program to run and revitalize the football program at Stillwater. Not having the freedom of naming his own staff for the 1971 season, George had little choice but to keep me on as an assistant, at least for the upcoming season. Thus began a working partnership that would play out over the next three decades.

Being the hockey coach at Stillwater High School fulfilled my ambitions of being a head coach, while my role in the football program was extensive, challenging and rewarding enough to overcome any thoughts of moving on to a head coaching position in that sport. In short, I was able to do what I had always wanted to do, teach young men the values of competition and team play and how to play the great game of football.

## Sharing the Wealth

I contend that in any profession, when workers are assigned specific job-related responsibilities and are made to feel that they are major players in the overall scheme of things, they will then perform at their highest level of proficiency. By the same token, additional worker incentives—such as profit sharing, matching funds, promotions from within and the like—are extra incentives to encourage not only loyalty and dedication, but also highly competent input. In the corporate world, the successful CEO will employ all of these methods and more to ensure that his company's stockholders and investors are pleased and satisfied that the business is being run smoothly and is in capable hands.

By shifting gears, it is interesting to apply the previously mentioned methods and criteria to the operation of our football staff at Stillwater Area High School between 1971 and 1999. Again, speaking in my own behest, allow me to cite why I believe we were a cohesive, viable force over that extended period of time.

Early on, with a small staff that included but three varsity and two sophomore coaches, our duties were vast and all encompassing. Lacking elaborate titles, our responsibilities included all special teams, along with coaching techniques on both sides of line of scrimmage. As our staff grew in numbers, coaching responsibilities became more concentrated and specialized, covering specific areas of the game. Labels such as offensive line coach, defensive line coach, secondary coach, linebackers and defensive ends coach and such were in vogue in the late 1970s and early 1980s. Soon, we were diversified into offensive and defensive staffs, working together as a unit to achieve the goals and objectives of the group. With the times came titles: special teams coach, defensive and offensive coordinators, all under the auspices and direction of the head coach.

Key factors that united our staff over the long haul are many. George conducted his program and staff in much the same fashion as any CEO would run a successful business. He was adroit in accessing the strengths and weaknesses of his coaches, placing them in areas of responsibility where they would be most likely to experience a high level of success and be of the greatest value to the program. Once George developed confidence in the ability of a coach, he didn't hesitate to delegate specific responsibilities to that coach and always expected these assignments to be carried out with enthusiasm and proficiency. George was careful not to assign a coach a responsibility or duty that he was incapable of carrying out and was patient enough to wean the young coaches slowly into the program, advancing them as they developed and gained confidence in their own abilities.

Though all coaching staffs work hard, put in long hours, and earn every penny of their salary, I don't believe any high school staff in the state of Minnesota worked harder than we did. In our preparation, no detail or facet of the game was left to chance. We felt going into the game each Friday night that we were totally prepared to handle any and all situations that might arise. Our players were conditioned "to expect the unexpected," not to panic if things didn't go our way, and never to lose sight of victory.

Table A-1 illustrates the continuity and longevity enjoyed by the Stillwater football coaching staff from the fall of 1971 through the 1999 season under coach Thole. The right-hand column shows our years together as a staff.

| Coach | Years of Coaching Experience | Years With Stillwater/Thole |
|---|---|---|
| George Thole | 34 | 29 |
| Jerry Foley | 39 | 29 |
| Dick Klein | 30 | 29 |
| Dennis Meyer | 22 | 22 |
| Scott Hoffman | 20 | 19 |
| Mike Pavlovich | 24 | 24 |
| Gary Gustafson | 41 | 6 |
| Joe Samuelson | 41 | 15 |
| Donn Drommerhausen | 27 | 27 |
| Tom Rasmussen | 27 | 27 |
| Mark Elmer | 12 | 12 |

Table A-1. Stillwater football coaching staff 1971-1999

In short, our staff enjoyed longevity because, as individuals, we were satisfied that each of us played a significant role in a very successful program. It is gratifying to be needed, appreciated, and to be a part of something good. The head coach was quick to recognize a job well done by his coworkers and wasn't hesitant to share the accolades that accompany success. Everyone in the program, from the scouts through the junior high coaches, along with our film crew and the chain gang, were included when celebrating the spoils of victory. The secretaries and cooks lined up for Stillwater t-shirts, while the grounds crew all sported the latest Pony coaching hats—prime examples of taking profit-sharing to the next level and making everyone happy.

My coaching career was prolonged because of my association with George. Not only did we have a bond that included a close friendship, we were able to work side by side, seeing eye to eye, while agreeing to disagree, accompanied by a demeanor that allowed our personalities to feed off each other. I relished the challenges and responsibilities that went along with the job of offensive coordinator, but wasn't burdened with the countless other duties and pressures that befall the head coach. The aspects of planning, formulating, and carrying out the offensive game plan on Friday night was always exciting and got the adrenaline moving. Making a critical call while being involved in game deciding decisions proved to be an enervating and rewarding experience. I am forever grateful for the opportunity. When the lights came up on game night, the competitive juices were flowing and I felt all of the sensations of excitement, pressure, and responsibility that anyone needs to satisfy the competitive spirit.

# Appendix B: Spit, Polish, and Other Stuff

**George Thole**

In writing a final chapter to this exercise in option football, we wanted to throw out some generalizations about our beloved game of football. For lack of a better description, this chapter will be a catchall, if nothing else. We assume that readers have been attending coaching clinics on a regular basis and keeping up with the changes in the game. Without sounding trite, we want to remind the reader that blocking and tackling are what ultimately win football games. Failure in these areas makes everything else a moot point.

## Coaching Today

You probably don't have to be told this, but coaching today is more difficult than at any other time in history. Coaches are dedicated people who put in far more hours than they are compensated for. They put themselves under pressure as they deal with the everyday stresses of coaching, with problems in their players' lives, and with the sometimes unrealistic expectations of parents (50 percent of parents think their kids should get college scholarships, while fewer than 5 percent actually will). Some people want you to win all the time, and others couldn't care less as long as their kid plays.

More demands are placed on coaches each year. Recruiting takes up more time than it once did due to changes in NCAA rules. College coaches must stay away from watching prospects play during the early part of the season. As a result, it's not unusual for 15 colleges per week to expect you to make video copies of your games. Doing so takes time, and you don't have any grad assistants to do it for you. It is all worth it, however, when you attend scores of weddings and have your former players take pride in introducing their offspring to you. A better job on this planet would be hard to find when you take time to really think about it.

## Law of the Jungle

Following is some sage advice to pass on to your players when two-a-day practices start next fall. Tell them to consider, while cavorting on the green grass, that every morning in Africa when a gazelle wakes up, it knows it must run faster than the fastest lion or be killed. Every morning a lion wakes up, and it knows it must outrun the slowest gazelle, or it will starve to death.

# Six Important Questions

Boys will be boys, and girls will be girls, and every year adolescents experiment with everything from illegal-substance use to sex, and this type of behavior causes havoc with high school athletic teams. We tell our athletes that if you assume the risk, then you must accept the consequences of your actions.

Furthermore, tobacco, alcohol, and drug rules apply to the whole school year. The most difficult time for teens usually occurs between the seasons or during the holidays. I recommend the following rules of thumb to gauge their thinking as to the wisdom of their actions. Tell athletes that before they head out to that party, they should ask themselves:

- Is this a risk I can afford?
- How will this affect my future?
- How will my parents feel about this?
- How will this reflect on my team and coaches?
- How does this represent my school?
- Am I surrounding myself with people who want me to succeed?

Every year, we see broken-hearted student-athletes and parents dealing with ineligibility. I tell them, "High school is an exciting time in your lives, so let's not mess it up. This is my last word on the subject. You know what's right, and you know what's wrong—do what's right."

# Rules and Philosophy

For any group to function, they must have clearly defined rules for the betterment of the organization. Following are some of the rules we have used:

- No putdowns. Nobody likes a putdown, and it is self-destructive.
- If a player has missed practice without an excuse on one occasion, he will be suspended from the squad. Call a coach and inform him beforehand; after-the-fact excuses just don't cut it.
- As coaches, we must assume that players abstain from tobacco, alcohol, and drugs. Therefore, stay away from people who use them. It includes staying away from parties where these substances will be present. Football players are high-esteem people; surround yourself with people who are like you.
- Pick your friends, but not to pieces. Do not consider yourself to be better than the so-called "non-athlete." He has feelings just like you do. Try to encourage people to be fans of football because we need their support. Seniors are not better than

sophomores, so treat them with respect. Sophomores are future varsity, so don't run any of them off.

- The locker room is no place for horseplay. Horseplay is for horses; our game is football. Keep the place clean, and treat it like a palace.
- Be a leader. A leader is a young man with a magnet in his heart and a compass in his head.
- Be a student. School comes first. We expect to hear only good things from your teachers.
- Always play with enthusiasm.
- Be loyal. When you go to the class reunion in 10 or 20 years, you will migrate toward your football buddies because you have a special bond. That's just the way it is.
- Hustle. Everyone can hustle 100 percent of the time, and it results in victories.

# Get Better, or Get Beaten

Back in the days when I was coaching, I always tried to figure out new ways to motivate our football players to play hard and accomplish things that even they didn't think were possible. In trying to better understand these teenage warriors, I would study tons of material on the mental aspects of performance. Many of these ideas were founded in logic, and after years of coaching experience, I found them to be accurate.

Even four years after retirement, I still manage to hit the speaking circuit a few times each year. The question I am asked the most is to describe the difference between athletes then and now. I always answer by stating that when I started coaching in 1965, the players were 16 to 18 years old, and when I left in 1999, they were still 16 to 18 years old. They didn't change much, but I did because I was 26 when I started and 60 when I departed.

At the start of each season, I would tell the varsity squad that it would be easier for the 80 of them to adjust to the one of me than vice versa. I coached that way for over three decades and would defiantly do it that way again. I am always being told by former players that they believe I was strong in the motivation department.

A coach must also keep a sharp eye on the athletes' grades and learn to cope with sometimes angry parents and alumni. While attending to these and many other demands on his psychological skills, the coach wants to win, because coaching success is often defined in terms of the coach's win-loss record. Some might say that winning isn't important, but tell that to your doctor, lawyer, salesman, policeman, or whomever. Winning is an attitude! My advice to all athletes and coaches is that if you want to be a champion, then get to work. Get better, or get beaten.

# Why Not Win?

Let's face it. We all want to win, or we wouldn't go through all the angst of coaching. This job is not easy, but it is the most rewarding, especially when you see improvement in your team's performance.

How many times have you heard the absurd "winning is not important" proclamation? We always responded with, "Okay, tell that to your doctor or lawyer, and take down that scoreboard because it's intimidating. I'm having brain surgery next week, so I'm going to a guy who finished at the bottom of his class at medical school to do the cutting."

We know the truth. If this is a competitive society, then we should teach our players how to win. Winning is important; losing isn't. In order to win, the coach must learn to deal with unrealistic parents, contend with teachers who don't share his views on football, and cope with the lovesick star player who has just been given the Grand Canyon treatment from his girlfriend.

Winning has a way of putting salve on these wounds and more bounce in the step. The bottom line is that if the coach doesn't win, he will join the multitude that has preceded him. The coach needs to win just as the salesman needs to sell.

# Three Types of Football Players

- *Smart*: This guy understands the concepts that he is being taught and has a high standard of character. He knows that a team must have discipline to be successful. He puts the welfare of the team first and follows all the rules—he's easy to coach.
- *Smarter than he thinks he is*: This kid has ability, but lacks self-confidence. He needs many positive strokes on his way to becoming a productive player.
- *Not as smart as he thinks he is*: This player will cause his coaches the most anguish. He is usually among the more talented players on the squad and is often on the edge of being a problem. He will need to have his demeanor tweaked by his coaches.

One day at practice, you will look around and see only smart players and a squad that is on the same page. Over several years of coaching, these observations pertained to every winning team. In pursuing the overall goal of winning, the coach is continuously confronted with situations that require skill in handling problem players.

# Reflections With the Retirees

I spoke to a group of retired coaches and officials at a banquet at the Knights of Columbus Hall. I told them the three types of coaches are: those who know what is going on, those who don't know what's going on, and those who don't even suspect anything is going on. (Just a few of us are in that last category, but we sure seem to win a lot.)

Next, I compared the difference between the equipment these men had played in, and the equipment used in the modern game. First of all, helmets were not state-of-the-art like they are today. Face guards were not used prior to 1953, and mouth guards were for wimps. You saw a lot of guys with broken noses and chipped teeth back in those days. Standards for helmets were unheard of, and they didn't offer the protection of today's models. I can't recall all the times I had my bell rung and had to be brought back around with smelling salts (a real no-no today).

We were not allowed water during practices, and some guys would carry a lemon in their socks (which we would all share). During games, the managers would bring out a bucket full of water and towels during time-outs. Some players would wipe their faces and throw the towels back in the bucket, and someone else would pick it up and suck the water out of it.

Football is the only pure sport, as it does not require a year-round regimen of playing games or participation in off-season leagues. Injuries are way down as a percentage of participants, as are catastrophic injuries. Even when the old-timers played with poor helmets, no water, no mouth guard, heavy cotton jerseys, and no common sense, it was a relatively safe activity.

I never scored a touchdown, but I did recover three fumbles and had an interception during my career (mostly high school). Football was good to me, but I never played on a championship team. Runner-up in my junior year in high school was as close as I would get. I did enjoy being a lineman because being a hitter is more fun than being a "hittee." My fervor for and appreciation of hogs is well documented, as they are the unknown soldiers.

Leaving football coaching was a tough decision because the game, except for the two years that I spent in the U.S. Navy, was a major part of my life every year since I was 15. Lifting a few words from South Carolina Coach Lou Holtz, we know that football is a replica of life. In no other sport do you get knocked down more than in football, which is also true in life. You just have to keep getting up with a more determined effort toward success. People respect courage much more than ability.

I owe a debt of gratitude for all the young men whom I have had the pleasure to coach. I was inducted into the North Dakota State University Athletic Hall of Fame, but we all know that it was based more on what the Stillwater Ponies did on the gridiron than anything that I did (we were 7-11-1, hardly the stuff that gets you into a college hall of fame).

Being on the radio did fill some of the void on Friday nights, but nothing beats the thrill of preparing a team for action. The soul-searching after a heartbreaking loss, when you bounce back with a more determined effort, and the thrill of victory are all parts that form the other half of education.

Do I miss coaching football? Heck, yes, I do! *Finis*.

# The Big Picture

A study by the NCAA revealed that for every single opening in professional sports, you will have 325 openings for teachers, 60 openings for physicians, 125 openings for physical therapists, 10 openings for architects, 75 openings for attorneys, 15 openings for dentists, 80 openings for computer programmers, 24 openings for librarians, and 40 openings for social workers. Get the picture?

Sometimes as parents, we see our kids in a different light than the coaches do. Our judgment is a little tainted and biased as parents. As a former head coach and parent, I know that moms and dads don't always see their children's abilities objectively. That's okay, because it's important for parents to believe that their children are special or unique. Just remember that the coach wants what's best for your children and sees them every day in practice and maybe has a more realistic view of their abilities. Work together with the coaches, and the rewards will be great. A pro contract or a college scholarship? I doubt it.

Remember that coaching is a complex process in which the psychological and spiritual qualities of the athlete sometimes require as much focus as the physical and strategic facets of the game. It is called motivation, and all athletes need it—some more than others, but no one is exempt. One of the most time-honored motivational appeals is nurtured in the home. Parental help is the best kind; just ask any coach.

It was interesting perusing an article by Kevin Merkle, associate director of the Minnesota State High School League, in its bulletin. He states that while a winning attitude is needed for success, a supportive attitude may be more important. When we talk about a winning attitude, we mean always preparing to win, always striving to win, and learning to expect to win. Winning will happen if the participants have the opportunity for sound practices and can play with others of comparable or superior ability. Merkle goes on to suggest that large numbers of participants are important so that talented athletes are available and can be developed and so that you have competition among players for starting positions.

The biggest kick that we got out of coaching was watching young athletes improve, grow, and then maximize their abilities. Don't get me wrong; winning certainly adds to the enjoyment that players, coaches, fans, and parents derive from the sport.

# The Little Things

I don't know where we picked up the following sage advice, but it was in our playbook for over 30 years. Sometimes, we get lost in minutia, but nevertheless, the "little" things should not be overlooked. Through the years, we've won several games because we knew the rulebook better than our opponents did.

The difference between winning and losing often hinges on some minute detail of play. This is especially true in games where teams are evenly matched and in the really big games where championships hang in the balance.

There is, therefore, no aspect of the game that is deemed too inconsequential to receive the necessary attention. The crucial situation is often decided by preparation in a relatively obscure aspect of the game of football. For example, knowledge or lack of knowledge of the rules can often result in the play that decided the game. The inability to conserve or to use time on the game clock often results in a loss, which could have been prevented.

The above are merely two examples of the importance of the "little" things, and do not seek to be all-inclusive here in discussing the importance of the "little" things.

It is granted that all the major high school football teams are well-prepared in the major departments of play. Their approach is sound, and their coaching is excellent. Thus, we acknowledge they are all good football teams.

There may be a number, however, who do not pay painstaking attention to a situation that might arise just once or twice in an entire season. Yet, when these situations do arise, the team that can cope with them best is the winner.

The difference between being good and being a champion is relatively small, but in order to gain that difference, an intense application of coaching effort and organization is needed. To the person in coaching, as a profession, no effort should loom as too great to make. The coach who neglects the details will have the job of convincing the world that he is a "tough luck" coach.

A thorough checklist, periodically referred to and occasionally revised, provides the starting point for an assurance that the "little" things will be successfully covered.

—Anonymous

# All "Squares" Please Stand

The following poem was recited by Macalester College Athletic Director Irv Cross, the former Northwestern University and Philadelphia Eagle football star who went on to fame as a TV celebrity at CBS. He first recited this nugget at an FCA meeting in Boston in April 1980.

"Square," another of the good old words, has gone the way of "love" and "modesty" and "patriotism."

Something to be snickered over or outright laughed at.

It used to be that there was no higher compliment you could pay a man than to call him a "square-shooter."

The adman's promise of a "square deal" once was as binding as an oath on the Bible.

One of those admen, Charles Brower, says he's fed up with this beat generation distorting and corrupting our time-honored vocabulary.

He said most of this first, but we second the motion.

Today's "square" is a guy who volunteers when he doesn't have to.

He's a guy who gets his kicks from trying to do a job better than anyone else.

He's a boob who gets so lost in his work he has to be reminded to go home,

A square is a guy who doesn't want to stop at the bar and get all juiced up because he prefers to go to his own home, his own dinner table, his own bed.

He hasn't learned to cut corners or goof off.

This creep we call a "square" gets all choked up when he hears children singing, "My country, 'tis of Thee…"

He even believes in God—and says so—in public!

Some of the old squares were Nathan Hale, Patrick Henry, Ben Franklin, George Washington.

Some of the new squares are Glenn, Shepard, Carpenter, Cooper, Schirra.

A square is a guy who lives within his means whether the Joneses do or not and thinks his Uncle Sam should, too.

A square is likely to save some of his own money for a rainy day rather than count on yours.

A square gets his books out of the library instead of the drugstore.

He tells his son it's more important to play fair than to win. Imagine!

A square is a guy who reads scripture when nobody's watching, prays when nobody's listening.

A guy who wants to see America first—in everything.

He believes in honoring father and mother and "do unto others" and that kind of stuff.

He thinks he knows more than his teenager knows about cars, freedom, and curfew.

Will all gooney birds answering this description, please stand up.

You misfits in this brave new age, you dismally disorganized, improperly apologetic ghosts of the past, stand up!

Stand up and be counted!

You squares…who turn the wheels and dig the fields and move mountains and put rivets in our dreams.

You squares…who dignify the human race.

You squares who hold the thankless world in place.

## Ode To George

When he came to this town where the water runs still
The great sport of football had never a thrill.
The Ponies started winning and in a few years
Touchdowns resulted and many loud cheers.
This program was based on the Ponies and pride
And a fella named George took us all for a ride.
He worked with his coaches to prepare for each test,
And at the end of each season the Ponies were best.
So good was the program they made every team say,
"Look out for the Ponies, let's get out of their way."
In '75, it seemed just like fate,
Things fell in place and the Ponies won State.
For the next 20 years this team tackled and scored
There were many a champion and at state we won four.
More important than wins was teamwork and pride,
The Ponies attacked and they took it in stride.
George taught the kids rules and skills of all sorts.
But more important than that he made them good sports.
To George, we are grateful, he helped the young men
To do the right things again and again.
So as we conclude a coach's great run,
Let's never forget: It's all about fun.
Thank you, George.

—John Bianchi,
Stillwater Area High School Principal, 1999

# About the Authors

**George Thole**, a native of Petaluma, California, received his bachelor's degree from North Dakota State University and his master's degree from Minnesota State University. He also did graduate work at the University of Minnesota. He taught for 33 years and has 32 years of head coaching experience with one of the most storied coaching careers in the upper Midwest. Thole played football at Petaluma California High School and North Dakota State University, where he was a two-way starter at guard and a hall-of-fame selection. He began his coaching career in 1965 at Central Cass High School in Casselton, North Dakota, where his teams compiled a 27-0 record.

Thole and his family moved to Stillwater in 1971. He spent 29 years teaching and coaching football at Stillwater Area High School, contributing to a lifetime coaching record of 285-69-2. His coaching accomplishments include four Minnesota state championships, two state runners-up, 18 state tournament appearances, 17 conference championships, and 12 sectional titles. Thole ranks third on Minnesota's all-time football victory list. Other personal achievements include 95 coaching awards, 13 community awards, and six hall-of-fame inductions. Thole has worked over 77 football clinics in six states during his career and is honored to be on staff or act as an advisor/chairman to organize and promote a variety of metro, state, and regional football affiliated clinics, committees, commissions, and charities.

Past president of the Minnesota State Football Coaches Association, Thole has coached all-star games in Minnesota and Ireland. He was host on the Friday Night Football Scoreboard Show (KSTP 1500 AM radio) in the Twin Cities from 2000 to 2003 and is a current member of the ISD 834 Board of Education. He remains actively involved in football with coaching clinics, speaking engagements, teaching classes on achieving peak performance, sports writing, and advising/reviewing training videos and documentary productions. Thole and his wife, Karen, currently reside in Stillwater, Minnesota. They have been married for 46 years and have two children: Eric, 42, and Kiersten, 38.

**Jerry Foley** has been recognized with the Butch Nash Award, Assistant Coach of the Year, and All-Star Coach by the Minnesota Football Coaches Association for his coaching accomplishments. He has been inducted into the Hamline University Athletic

Hall of Fame, the Minnesota Old-Timers Football Hall of Fame, the Humboldt High School Athletic Hall of Fame, and the St. Croix Valley Sports Hall of Fame.

As a collegiate quarterback, Foley won two national titles (NCAA III), leading the nation in both passing and total offense for the 1955 football season. In doing so, he set many national passing records, along with numerous conference and school records, and virtually rewrote the Hamline record book for passing statistics and total offense. Foley's 33 completions against St. John's University on October 8, 1955, were national, state, and conference records. His 62 attempts, without interception, was also a national record. Among the many accolades that Foley received as a quarterback at Hamline University, being named to the Williamson Small College All-America Football Team (Honorary Mention) in 1955 ranks high on his list of accomplishments as a student athlete. He was named the Hamline University Alumni Football Coach of the Year for his many contributions to high school football.

In 1990, Foley was selected as a coach in the Minnesota High School All-Star Football Game, sponsored and managed by the M.H.S.F.C.A. He received his profession's highest award when he was chosen as the Assistant Football Coach of the Year for the state of Minnesota in 1990. Upon his retirement, Stillwater Area High School honored Foley with the Jim McLaughlin Coach's Award in the spring of 2000. Throughout Foley's teaching and coaching career and into retirement, he has participated in numerous football and sports clinics and speaking engagements, and he has been a valuable resource for area teams in need of his expertise as a football clinician. Foley and his wife, Darlene, live in Stillwater, Minnesota, and are looking forward to watching the exploits of their multitude of grandchildren provided by Brian Foley, Colleen Halverson, and Kathlene Junker.